The Complete
Helen Reddy
Illustrated
Discography

Daniel Selby

Note: Many foreign 45 releases were issued with the same catalog # and picture sleeves for different countries, especially neighboring. Also some were re–issued with a different design / number at a later time. Not all are presented here. Nor are all Greatest Hits, Best Of or similar compilation albums documented. Album release dates, recording dates and other information researched through Billboard and Cashbox magazines / websites, press releases and Capitol Records archives. I have not listed all chart statistics for every release. In addition release dates will tend to be U.S. dates and foreign dates may differ, unless it is a foreign only release of course. Not all re-issues (single or LP) are listed. I have strived to be as accurate as possible, but occasionally mistakes make it through. If found, please send corrections (with sources) to me through: bookwriter@gmail.com.

Published in the USA and abroad by:

BEARMANOR MEDIA

New books on classic stars.

www.bearmanor–digital.myshopify.com/

Cover Layout & Interior Design:
From Design to Done Graphics / Daniel Selby

ISBN: 978-1-62933-784-5

Special Thanks

First, I would like to thank **Helen Reddy**. A person who was so giving of herself when I was around her. A person who gave so much to the world of music and loved sharing her talent. Someone who was also fiercely determined to succeed, "can't" was never part of her vocabulary. When we last met in Des Moines, Iowa in 2010 I asked her about critics and people who didn't like her. "Oh honey, you can't worry about *those* people," she said during dinner, "If all they can do is find your supposed faults, you're better off ignoring them! There will always be some people who won't like *anything* you do! Don't listen to critics... *who* are they after all? You need to simply do the best you possibly can and then forget it. Never worry about what reviews or critics say, good or bad. If *you're* happy with what you've done then that is all that matters!" Well, I am happy with this book and while Helen did not live to see it finished I think she would have been happy with it as well. I had presented her with a smaller, less elaborate Helen Reddy discography book some years ago and she was tickled. She loved history. I am thankful she left such a legacy of music for us to continue to enjoy. I love and miss you Helen!

To **Allan** for *always* supporting me and my writing and other creative projects. Also for all the love the last 34 years.

Thank you to **worldradiohistory.com/** for all the back copies of Billboard, Cashbox, Record World and other industry magazines that helped *tremendously* with research of chart placement, sales, release dates, recording dates, studios used, reviews and interview quotes.

Helen...

I am terribly saddened over the fact that Helen suffered with dementia, a horrible disease that my mother now suffers with. The fact that Helen may have lost the ability to remember all she accomplished with her music is heartbreaking. Yet, I am joyful in the fact that she has left us with her music. Those magnetic pulses left on studio tape have brought **so** many people happiness the world over. Some will like this book, some will not. But as Helen told me about critics; "Oh honey, you can't worry about **those** people..." so I won't. I am happy with this book and I did the best I could, which Helen also said is the best you can do. It is with those thoughts that I dedicate this book to the one who made it possible; Helen Reddy.

Helen with the author on November 16, 2010 in Des Moines, Iowa. Helen had come to give a speech and this photo was taken after the dinner beforehand. She asked that I get close to her and that my agent try to crop out our dinner dishes! When she had time Helen enjoyed walking around cities that she visited and several of us walked around downtown Des Moines ahead of the dinner and her speech. I have my agent to thank for setting this up and for taking the photo after dinner. I asked Helen a lot about her career and her records. She signed an album for me that night. A wonderful person who _never_ lost her inner *or* outer beauty!

A Little About
Helen Reddy

Helen Maxine Reddy was born into a well-known Australian show-business family on October 25, 1941 in Melbourne. Her mother was actress, singer, and dancer Stella Campbell (née Lamond) (born March 12, 1909 in Sydney, New South Wales, Australia, died July 5, 1973 in Melbourne, Victoria, Australia) and father, writer, producer, and actor Maxwell David "Max" Reddy (born 1914 in Melbourne, Victoria, died on September 13, 1973). Her mother was known to perform often at the Majestic Theatre in Sydney but was perhaps best known as a regular cast member on the television programs *Homicide* (1964), *Bellbird* (1967) and *Country Town* (1971). Helen also had a half-sister Toni Lamond who was a professional singer.

At the young age of four, Helen joined her parents on the Australian vaudeville tours, singing and dancing; she recalled: "It was instilled in me: *You will be a star*. So between the ages of 12 and 17, I got rebellious and decided this was not for me. I was going to be a housewife and mother." At age 12, due to her parents' constant touring nationwide as well as their increasing arguments, Helen went to live with her paternal aunt, Helen "Nell" Reddy "... who was her namesake as well as someone she looked up to. Her aunt gave Helen the stability, a sense of morality, and the strength she would need for her future as a singer-songwriter who motivated women. The young Helen's teen revolt in favor of domesticity culminated in the marriage to Kenneth Claude Weate, a considerably older musician and family friend. The marriage did produce a daughter, but unfortunately the union did not fare well and the couple divorced. Helen now found herself a single mother in need of income. So, to support herself and daughter Traci, she revitalize her performing career, concentrating on singing. She sang everywhere— on radio and television, eventually winning the top prize in a talent contest on the Australian show *Bandstand*, the prize being a trip to New York City to cut a single for Mercury Records and some cash. Upon arrival in New York in 1966, Helen was advised that her prize was only the chance to try out for the label and that Mercury considered the *Bandstand* footage to be her audition, which they deemed unsatisfactory. Though having only $200 and a return ticket to Australia, Helen decided to remain in the United States with 3-year-old Traci and pursue a singing career. Can't was *not* in her vocabulary.

Regrettably her lack of a work permit made it difficult to get singing jobs in the US, and she was forced to make trips back and forth to Canada, which did not require work permits for citizens of Commonwealth countries, in order to make some money. In 1967, Martin St. James, an Australian stage hypnotist that she had met and befriended while in New York City, threw Helen a party with an admission price of $5 to enable Helen, who was down to her last $12, to be able to pay her rent. At this social occasion, Helen met her future manager and husband, Jeff Wald, a 22-year-old secretary at the William Morris Agency, who had crashed the affair. Helen told *People Magazine* in 1975; "Jeff didn't pay the five dollars, but it was love at first sight."

Jeff has stated that he and Helen married three days after meeting, (though Helen refutes this saying she was still legally married to Kenneth), and along with daughter Traci, the couple moved into the Hotel Albert in Greenwich Village. Helen later said that she married Jeff out of desperation over her inability to work and live in the United States. According to *New York Magazine*, Jeff was fired from the William Morris Agency soon after having met Helen, and so Helen supported them for six months doing $35-a-night hospital and charity benefit shows. Helen has said about the time, "When we did eat, it was spaghetti, and we spent what little extra money we had on cockroach spray." In September of 1967 they left New York for Chicago and Jeff landed a job as talent coordinator at Mister Kelly's. While in Chicago, Helen gained a reputation for singing in the local lounges, including Mister Kelly's, and in 1968 she landed a deal with Fontana Records, a division of major Chicago-based label Mercury Records. Her first single, "One Way Ticket," on Fontana was not a US hit, but it did give Helen her first appearance on any chart— it peaked at number 83 in her native Australia.

The following year, 1969, Jeff moved Helen and Traci to Los Angeles, where he was hired by Capitol Records, the label under which Helen was to attain stardom; however, he was hired and fired the same day for reasons unknown. At the same time, in 1969, Helen had enrolled at the University of California Los Angeles to study psychology and philosophy part-time.

Helen became frustrated as Jeff began to successfully promote other acts such as Deep Purple and Tiny Tim without putting any obvious effort into promoting her. After enduring 18 months of career inactivity, Helen gave Jeff an ultimatum, he either regenerate her career or get out. He knew she was serious.

Fortunately around that time Flip Wilson was filling in for Johnny Carson on The Tonight Show and he asked Helen to be on the show as a guest. Flip and Helen had met in Chicago years before and became friends. They also supported each other whenever they could. Capitol Records executive Artie Mogull saw the program and offered Helen a contract to cut two songs for a 45 single. However, there was a stipulation to the contract, Helen had to record "I Don't Know How To Love Him" as one of the songs. It was Jeff who broached the song idea suggested by Artie. Helen was not happy with that idea, but felt she had to go along with Artie if she wanted to record at all. This could be her last chance to make a record.

In late November, early December 1970 Helen entered A&M Recording Studios, Studio D to cut "I Believe in Music" written by Mac Davis whom she had seen sing the song on a late night talk show backed with "I Don't Know How to Love Him" from Tim Rice and Andrew Lloyd Webber's *Jesus Christ Superstar*. Once released on January 4, 1971 Side A failed to do much on the charts, but several astute Canadian DJs turned the record over and that side became the hit, climbing up to number 13 in June 1971. Helen Reddy was on the rise with a song she really hadn't cared for.

However Helen's stardom was ultimately solidified in December 1972 when her single "I Am Woman" reached number one on the *Billboard Hot 100* chart. The song was co-written by Helen and fellow Aussie Ray Burton. Helen explained the drive for writing "I Am Woman" was that she was looking for songs to record for her first album that reflected the positive self-image she had gained from being a part of the women's movement but could not find any, so "I realized that the song I was looking for didn't exist, and I was going to have to write it myself." The song was merely an album cut.

However, "I Am Woman" was re-recorded and released in May 1972 after the original version was used in a film called "Stand Up and Be Counted" and Capitol wanted to be ahead in the game should the film be a big hit. The song barely made it onto the charts. However soon enough female listeners took notice of the song and it slowly became an anthem for them everywhere. They began requesting it from their local radio stations in huge numbers resulting in its September chart re-entry and ultimate peak at number one that December. The song earned Helen a Grammy Award for Best Female Pop Vocal Performance. At the awards ceremony, Helen ended her acceptance speech by famously thanking God "...because *She* makes everything possible." The success of "I Am Woman" made Helen the first Australian singer to top the US charts and the first to win a Grammy.

Three decades after her Grammy, Helen said of the song's iconic status: "I think it came along at the right time. I'd gotten involved in the women's movement, and there were a lot of songs on the radio about being weak and being dainty and all those sort of things. All the women in my family, they were strong women. They worked. They lived through the Depression and a world war, and they were just strong women. I certainly didn't see myself as being dainty," she said.

Over the next five years following her first success, Helen released more than a dozen U.S. top-40 hits, including two more number-one hits. These tracks included "Peaceful" (# 12), "Delta Dawn" (# 1), "Leave Me Alone (Ruby Red Dress)" (# 3), "Keep on Singing" (# 15), "You and Me Against the World" (featuring daughter Traci reciting the spoken bookends - # 9), "Angie Baby" (# 1), "Emotion" (# 22), "Ain't No Way to Treat a Lady" (# 8), and "Somewhere in the Night" (# 19; three years later, a bigger hit for Barry Manilow when he took it to # 9 in the US, but only # 81 in Australia).

On July 23, 1974, Helen received a star on the Hollywood Walk of Fame for her work in the music industry. Appropriately enough it is located at 1750 Vine Street— right in front of Capitol

Records.

Helen was also instrumental in supporting the career of friend and fellow Aussie, Olivia Newton-John, encouraging her to move from England to the United States in the early 1970s, saying there were opportunities here for her that did not exist in the United Kingdom. Olivia took Helen's advice. One opportunity took place at a party Helen held at her house in late 1976. A chance meeting with Allan Carr, a film producer, lead to Olivia doing a screen test and then being cast as "Sandy" in a co-starring role in the hit film version of the musical *Grease*.

As the 1970's wound down Helen's chart performance faltered and she left Capitol Records in 1980 only to sign with MCA soon after. Under MCA Helen was not able to recapture the winning streak she had for so many years. Her records were not promoted as well as they could have been and her career was mismanaged as well.

In September 1981, Helen reported that she would be working on a pilot for her own TV sitcom series. In the unnamed show she would play a single mother working as a lounge singer in Lake Tahoe, but the pilot was never produced and no reason was ever given as to why. Helen took to doing theater touring, mostly in musicals. Some of her roles included:

Anything Goes – as "Reno Sweeney"
Sacramento Music Circus (July, 1985)
Long Beach Civic Light Opera (July, 1987)

Call Me Madam – as "Mrs. Sally Adams"
Sacramento Music Circus (August 11 - August 17, 1986)

The Mystery of Edwin Drood – as "Edwin Drood/Miss Alice Nutting"
Sacramento Music Circus (July, 1988)

Blood Brothers – as "Mrs. Johnstone"
Music Box Theatre, Broadway (January – May 1995)
Empire Theatre, Liverpool (1995)
West End (1997)

Love, Julie – as "Gail Sinclair"
Westport Country Playhouse (June,1996)
Cape Cod (July, 1996)
Sharon Stage, CT (August, 1996)

Shirley Valentine- as "Shirley"
Theatre by the Sea, R.I. (1995)
12 U.S. City Tour (February – April 1996)
Stage West, Canada (June,1997)

Helen would retire from performing in 2002. She returned to Australia and earned her degree, then practiced as a clinical hypnotherapist and motivational speaker giving talks the world over. In 2011, after singing "Breezin' Along with the Breeze" with her half-sister, Toni Lamond at Toni's birthday party, she decided to return to live performing and did for a while. Helen was diagnosed with dementia in 2015 and a while later moved into the Motion Picture & Television Hospital and Retirement Home in Los Angeles, California.

A film based on Helen's life and book was produced with the title *I Am Woman*. The film had its world premiere at the Toronto International Film Festival on September 5, 2019. Helen screened the film with director Unjoo Moon who reported that Helen sang along to her songs and cried at the end.

On September 29, 2020 Helen Reddy died at age 78. She was cremated and her ashes were scattered at sea. Helen was not afraid of dying. She said for her it was "returning home" or going back to "where one came from." I know she must be happy.

Awards & Nominations

Grammy Award
Best Female Pop Vocal Performance 1973.
Helen was nominated in this category in 1975 for her recording of "Ain't No Way To Treat A Lady."

American Music Award
Favorite Female Artist Pop/Rock 1974. Helen was also nominated in this category in 1975, 1976 and 1977.

Golden Globe
Helen was nominated for a Golden Globe for her role in *Airport 1975* in 1974.

People's Choice Awards
Helen was nominated in 1975 under the category of *Favorite Female Performer.*

ARIA Music Awards
In 2006 Helen was inducted into the **ARIA Hall of Fame** in Australia

AWMA Honour Roll
In 2018, the year it commenced, Helen was inducted in the Australian Women in Music Awards.

APRA Awards
In 2021 Helen was post-posthumously awarded the *Ted Albert Award* for Outstanding Services to Australian Music.

Special Recognition
In the December 2020 issue, Helen was listed at number 35 in Rolling Stone Australia's *50 Greatest Australian Artists of All Time.*

Some Facts:

- Helen was the first Australian to win a Grammy.
- Helen has sold over 25 million albums world-wide and 10 million singles in her career.
- Helen's song *Candle on the Water*, from Disney's *Pete's Dragon* was nominated for an Oscar.
- In 1974 Helen became a naturalized American citizen. She resumed her Australian citizenship when the opportunity to maintain dual American–Australian citizenship became available.
- Helen was a Democrat and very active in community affairs: In the 1970s she helped raise millions of dollars for Democratic Party political candidates. In July 1977, California Governor Jerry Brown appointed her to the nine-member commission overseeing the California Department of Parks and Recreation. Her nomination was unanimously approved. She served on the commission until she left in 1980.
- Helen's final public appearance was at the Los Angeles Women's March in January 2017. The music icon was introduced by Jamie Lee Curtis and sang the a capella version of "I Am Woman." Some footage was used in the film *Senior Entourage.*
- Helen served as the semi-regular host of NBC's "The Midnight Special."
- Helen was the only female performer that Frank Sinatra invited to perform at a star-studded benefit for Cedars-Sinai Hospital in Fall of 1974.
- Helen's version of "One Way Ticket" was sampled in 1999 in the Fatboy Slim and Freddy Fresh song "Badder Badder Schwing."

- Though a soundtrack album was released of *Airport 1975* by MCA (Cat. # MCA-2082 / US) and Helen sang a song (Best Friend) in the film, that track does not appear on the album. But a single was released in Japan of Helen's original 1971 track "Best Friend" with "Crazy Love" on the flip side to tie in with the film. These same tracks had been issued in Japan in reverse order on Capitol in 1971 with a picture sleeve (Cat. # CR-2885).
- In 1976, Helen recorded the Beatles' song "The Fool on the Hill" for the musical documentary *All This and World War II*.
- In April 2015, Helen released a cover of the Beatles' "All You Need Is Love" for the album *Keep Calm and Salute the Beatles* on the Purple Pyramid label.
- In 1978, Helen sang as a backup singer on Gene Simmons's solo album on the track "True Confessions."
- Among Helen's 20 Hot 100 Chart entries, six reached the top 10. Here's a look at her top Hot 100 hits:

Rank, Title, Peak Position, Peak Date
1. "Delta Dawn," No. 1, Sept. 15, 1973
2. "I Am Woman," No. 1, Dec. 9, 1972
3. "Angie Baby," No. 1, Dec. 28, 1974
4. "Leave Me Alone (Ruby Red Dress)," No. 3, Dec. 29, 1973
5. "You and Me Against the World," No. 9, Sept. 7, 1974
6. "Ain't No Way to Treat a Lady," No. 8, Oct. 11, 1975
7. "Peaceful," No. 12, May 5, 1973
8. "You're My World," No. 18, July 23, 1977
9. "I Don't Know How to Love Him," No. 13, June 5, 1971
10. "Somewhere in the Night," No. 19, Feb. 14, 1976

- In 2007, Helen had a voice cameo as herself in the *Family Guy* television show's *Star Wars* parody; "Blue Harvest."
- In 2011, Helen guest-starred on *Family Guy where she* sang the opening theme song for the show's fictional Channel 5 News telecast.
- Helen loved *Tim-Tams*. These can be found at most US Target stores in the cookie section.
- For as much as Helen conquered, "I Am Woman" was viewed as too controversial to be used at the April 15, 2018 Closing Ceremony of the Commonwealth Games in Australia!
- Helen appears on the 1987 Jessica Williams dance Maxi-single "Mysterious Kind" in which she provides background vocals.

The
Albums

→

I Don't Know How To Love Him
ST-762

Track Listing:
Crazy Love / How Can I Be Sure / Our House / I Am Woman / L.A. Breakdown / A Song for You / Don't Make Promises / I Believe in Music / Best Friend / I Don't Know How to Love Him

Production Information:
Produced by: Larry Marks
Recorded at: A&M Recording Studios and Capitol Studios, Los Angeles, CA
Engineered By: Hugh Davis / Ray Gerhardt

Singles Released From This Album:
"I Don't Know How To Love Him" b/w "I Believe in Music" - January 4, 1971(peaked at # 13 in the US on the Hot 100 Singles chart and # 10 in Canada on the *RPM* chart)
"Crazy Love" b/w "Best Friend" (peaked at # 51 in the US on the Hot 100 Singles chart and # 35 in Canada on the *RPM* chart)

Album Data:
Billboard Chart Debut: June 5, 1971
Highest Chart Position: 100
Billboard Chart: Top 200 Albums
Number of weeks on Chart: 37

Notes / Trivia:
- This album was released on LP, 8-Track and Cassette on May 10, 1971
- Sessions for the album took place between February and March 1971. The session for *I Don't Know How To Love Him* and *I Believe In Music* was held in early December 1970.
- This album contains the first recorded version of "I Am Woman." Helen would re-record the song for the 1972 *I Am Woman* album. The second version was re-arranged and partially re-written.
- In 1974, Reddy appeared in the film *Airport 1975*. As the character of Sister Ruth, Helen performed a solo acoustic version of "Best Friend" to an ailing passenger played by Linda Blair.
- In 2009 EMI Music Special Markets released a 12 track CD titled *Rarities from the Capitol Vaults* This disc included a country style arrangement of "I Am Woman."
- Album dedicated to Helen's then husband, Jeff Wald.
- The album cover was shot on Argyle Avenue right under the 101 Freeway with vines growing up the embankment and creeping up towards the underside of the road. This is just just blocks away from the Capitol Records office building. The vines have mostly died off during the ensuing 50 years and the area is strewn with trash.

- The album was certified gold on November 27, 1974.
- This album peaked at # 40 on Canada's RPM Chart.
- Liner notes by Lillian Roxon, author of "Rock Encyclopedia"
- The song *I Am Woman* was also used in Jim Fall's 1999 romantic comedy film "Trick." It was sung by Jessica Williams and lip-snyced by Miss Coco Peru in the film.
- On March 29, 2005 the album was released on CD for the first time along with Helen's follow up album *Helen Reddy* by the now defunct label *Raven Records* out of Australia. The label folded in April 2017.

**I Don't Know How To Love Him LP cover art from Holland.
Has 3/4 gate-fold cover with a bio and Helen's 2nd album featured on the interior.
(Catalog # 5C 054-80910)**

Helen Reddy
ST-857

Track Listing:
Time / How / Come On John / Summer of '71 / I Don't Remember My Childhood / No Sad Songs / I Think It's Going To Rain Today / Tulsa Turnaround / More Than You Could Take / New Year's Resovolution

Production Information:
Produced by: Larry Marks
Recorded at: Capitol Recording Studios, Hollywood, CA
Engineer: Hugh Davis
Cover Photography: Don Peterson
Art Direction: John Hoernle

Musicians:
Drums: Ron Tutt / John Payne Guerin / Russ Kunkel
Piano: Paul Parrish / Craig Doerge / Tom Hensley / Larry Knechtel
Electric Guitar: Larry Carlton
Bass: Leland Sklar / Jerry Scheff / Jack Conrad / Joe Osborne
Steel Guitar: Sneaky Pete Kleinow
Guitars: David Cohen / Dennis Budimir / Dean Parks / John Brennan / Larry Carlton
Mandolin: Larry Carlton
Percussion: Milt Holland
Accordion: Nick DeCaro
Special material arranged by: Nick DeCaro (strings) / Bob Thompson (piano)

Artist management: DeBlasio & Wald, Inc.

Singles Released From This Album:
"No Sad Song" b/w "More Than You Could Take" - November 1971 (peaked at # 62 in the US on the Hot 100 Singles chart in January 1972 and # 51 in Canada on the *RPM* chart)

Album Data:
Billboard Chart Debut: December 4, 1971
Highest Chart Position: 167
Billboard Chart: Top 200 Albums
Number of weeks on Chart: 7

Notes / Trivia:
- This album was released on LP, 8-Track and Cassette November 8, 1971.
- Sessions took place between August and September 1971.

- In 2009 EMI Music Special Markets released *Rarities from the Capitol Vaults*, a 12-track CD of mostly previously unreleased Helen Reddy recordings. One of which is "Plus De Chansons Tristes," the French version of "No Sad Song" that was only released in France.
- For many years this album was not well known by Helen's many, many fans. Thankfully since the 1990's the internet has made searching titles much easier.
- This album was re-issued in Australia in late February 1978 by World Record Club (Cat. # R 04238) with a 1977 cover photograph and titled "I Think It's Going To Rain Today."

The single for "No Sad Song" / "More Than You Could Take" from the Netherlands.

I Am Woman
ST-11068

Track Listing:
Peaceful / I Am Woman* / This Masquerade / I Didn't Mean To Love You / Where Is My Friend / And I Love You So / What Would They Say / Where Is The Love / Hit The Road Jack / The Last Blues Song

Production Information:
Produced by: Tom Catalano *except: Jay Senter
Recorded at: Sound Labs, Inc, Hollywood, CA / *except: Sunwest Recording Studios, Hollywood, CA
Engineer: Armin Steiner / *except: Buck Herring

Musicians for the track "I Am Woman" only:
Drums: Jim Gordon
Guitars: Mike Deasy
Piano: Mike Melvoin
Bass: Leland Sklar
Trombone: Dick Hyde
Saxophone: Don Menza
Background Vocals: Kathy Deasy, Clydie King, Venetta Fields and Shirley Matthews.
String & horn arrangements: Jim Horn
Arranger and conductor: Artie Butler

Artist management: Jeff Wald

Singles Released From This Album:
"I Am Woman" b/w "More Than You Could Take" - May 22, 1972 (peaked at # 1 in the US on the Hot 100 Singles chart and # 1 in Canada on the *RPM* chart)
"Peaceful" b/w "What Would They Say" - January 29, 1973 (peaked at # 12 in the US on the Hot 100 Singles chart and # 12 in Canada on the *RPM* chart)

Album Data:
Billboard Chart Debut: December 9, 1972
Highest Chart Position: 14
Billboard Chart: Top 200 Albums
Number of weeks on Chart: 62

Notes / Trivia:
- This album was released on LP, 8-Track, Quad 8-Track and Cassette on November 13, 1972.
- Sessions took place on April 23, 1972: "I Am Woman" / September 20, 1972: "This Masquerade" "Where Is My Friend," "And I Love You So" and "Where Is the Love" / October 9,

1972: "Peaceful," "I Didn't Mean to Love You" and "What Would They Say" / October 10, 1972: "Hit the Road, Jack" and "The Last Blues Song." String and horn overdub sessions followed each original session.

- The B side of the 1st single was pulled from Helen's previous Capitol album *Helen Reddy*.
- In Europe the B side of the 1st single is "Summer of '71."
- The US single of "I Am Woman" was certified gold on December 18, 1972 for one million+ copies sold.
- The album was certified gold on March 7, 1973 for sale in excess of 500,000 copies sold and it was certified platinum for one million copies sold on December 5, 1991.
- The song "I Am Woman" won a Grammy for Helen who made history when accepting the award by ending her thank you speech with "... and I thank God because *She* makes everything possible!" which caused a furor among religious fundamentalists.
- On July 22, 2003 this album was released for the first time on CD on a 2 on 1 disc along with the following album 1973's *Long Hard Climb*. And again in 2020 in the Hi-res Stereo / Quad format on a SACD by Vocalion.
- The original recording of "I Am Woman" was used in the 1972 film *Stand Up and Be Counted*.
- In the December 2, 1972 *Record World* issue the review read: "Title cut is streaking to the top of the charts, and this album has a good chance to do the same. Ms. Reddy touches on a wide variety of musical styles, with the old-timey "The Last Blues Song" of particular interest."

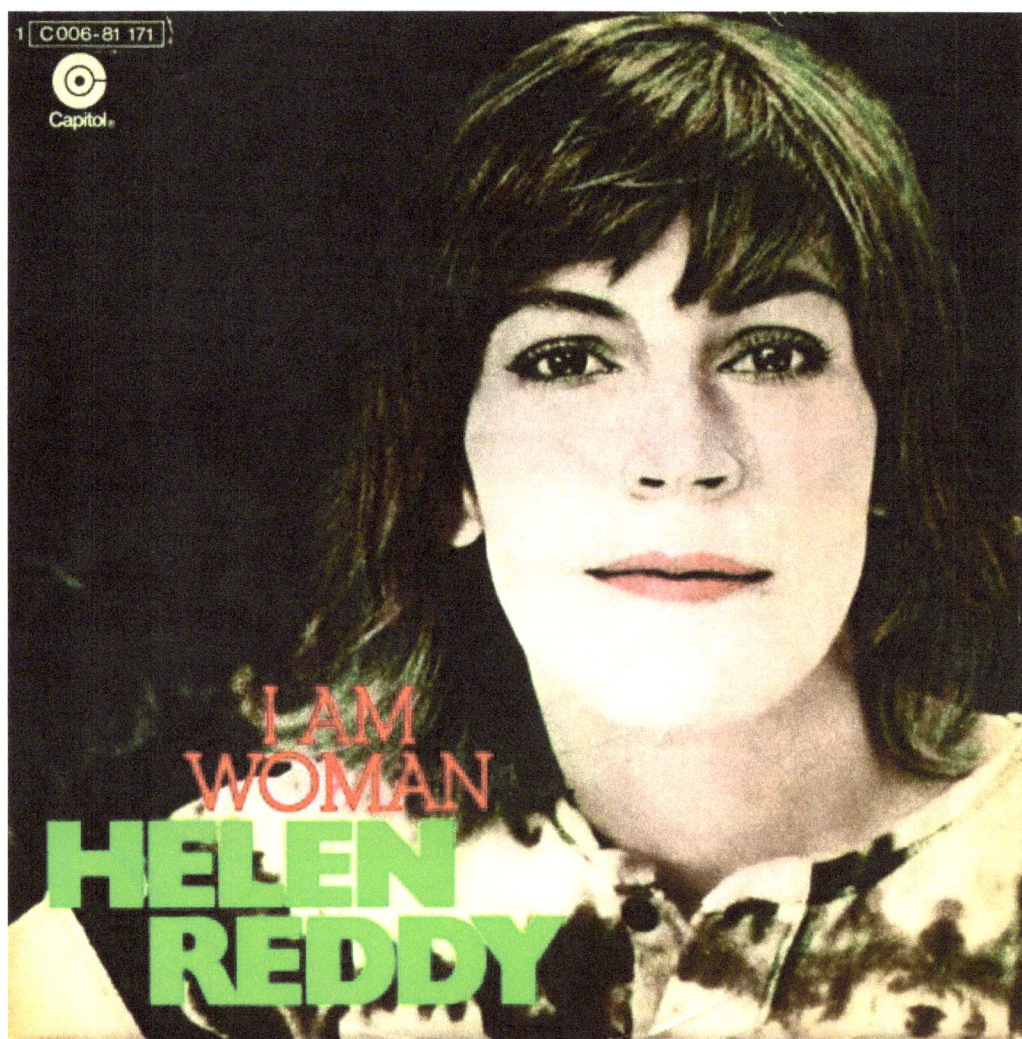

The single for "I Am Woman" / "Summer of '71" from the Netherlands

Long Hard Climb
ST-11213

Track Listing:
Leave Me Alone (Ruby Red Dress) / Lovin' You / A Bit OK / Don't Mess With A Woman* / Delta Dawn / The West Wind Circus / If We Could Still be Friends / Long Hard Climb / Until It's Time For You To Go / The Old fashioned Way

Production Information:
Produced by:Tom Catalano / *except: Jay Senter
Recorded at: Sound Labs, Hollywood, CA / *except: Sunwest Studios, Hollywood, CA.
Engineers: Armin Steiner / *except: Buck Herring
LP Mastered by: Doug Sax at The Mastering Lab, Los Angeles, CA
Cover Photography: Norman Seeff
Art Direction: John Hoernle

Singles Released From This Album:
"Delta Dawn" b/w "If We Could Still Be Friends" - June 11, 1973 (peaked at # 1 in the US on the Hot 100 Singles chart and # 1in Canada on the *RPM* chart)
"Leave Me Alone" (Ruby red Dress) b/w "The Old Fashioned way" - October 29, 1973 (peaked at # 3 in the US on the Hot 100 Singles chart and # 5 in Canada on the *RPM* chart)

Album Data:
Billboard Chart Debut: August 11, 1973
Highest Chart Position: 8
Billboard Chart: Top 200 Albums
Number of weeks on Chart: 43

Notes / Trivia:
- This album was released on LP, 8-Track, Quad 8-Track and Cassette on July 23, 1973.
- On August 30, 1973 the single "Delta Dawn" was certified gold for sales of 1,000,000 copies sold.
- On September 19, 1973 the album was certified gold for sales of 500,000+ copies.
- Of the song "Leave Me Alone (Ruby Red Dress)" Helen has said that it was "...one song I will never, *ever* sing again." Mentioning that it was its lyrical repetitiousness being the reason "...that sort of songwriting doesn't do much for me, but it was a hit. However, I don't have to sing it anymore if I don't want to... and I don't want to." The song was the subject of a nationwide contest in America in which listeners would submit to their local radio station their estimation of how many times Reddy sang the phrase "leave me alone" in the song; submissions of the correct answer - which Helen has said is 43 - were eligible for a trip for two to see Helen in concert.

- In 2009 EMI Music Special Markets released the CD *Rarities from the Capitol Vaults.* A 12-track disc which includes an alternate version of "Don't Mess with a Woman." This track was recorded at the same session as the re-recorded version of I Am Woman on April 23, 1972 at Sunwest Studios in Hollywood, CA..
- The single "Leave Me Alone (Ruby Red Dress)" / "The Old Fashioned Way" was certified gold on January 8, 1974 for sales of over 1,000,000 copies.
- This album along with the previous release, *I Am Woman*, have been reissued in a quad format on one disc by Vocalion in 2020. Hi-res stereo and quad mixes on SACD. These two albums had also bee released in quad format on LP and tape upon initial release.
- The album was re-issued on the green Capitol label without the tri-fold cover (Cat#. SN-16101).

**The single for "Leave Me Alone (Ruby Red Dress)" / "The Old Fashioned Way"
from Germany**

Love Song For Jeffrey
SO-11284

Track Listing:

That Old American Dream / You're My Home / Songs / I Got A Name / Keep On Singing / You And Me Against The World / Ah, My Sister / Pretty, Pretty / Love Song For Jeffrey / Stella By Starlight

Production Information:

Produced by: Tom Catalano
Recorded at: Sound Labs, Inc, Hollywood, CA
Engineer: Armin Steiner
Cover and Liner Photography: Virgil Mirano
Art Direction: Roy Kohara

Artists Management: Jeff Wald

Singles Released From This Album:

"Keep On Singing" b/w "You're My Home" - February 25, 1974 (peaked at # 15 in the US on the Hot 100 Singles chart and # 10 in Canada on the *RPM* chart)
"You And Me Against The World" b/w "Love Song For Jeffrey" - May 27, 1974 (peaked at # 9 in the US on the Hot 100 Singles chart and # 9 in Canada on the *RPM* chart)

Album Data:

Billboard Chart Debut: April 20, 1974
Highest Chart Position: 11
Billboard Chart: Top 200 Albums
Number of weeks on Chart: 25

Notes / Trivia:

- This album was released on LP, 8-Track, Quad 8-Track and Cassette on March 25, 1974.
- Helen dedicates the album to family that had died in the last year; "*In memory of my mother, Stella Lamond Reddy, July 1973, my father, Max Reddy, September 1973, and my beloved aunt, Helen Reddy Sr., January 1974; this album is lovingly and gratefully dedicated.*"
- The album was certified gold on June 6, 1974.
- On January 27, 2004, the album was released on CD as a 2 on 1 disc along with the following album *Free and Easy*.
- In 2009 EMI Music Special Markets released *Rarities from the Capitol Vaults*, a 12-track CD of mostly previously unreleased Helen Reddy recordings. One of which is an alternate take of the song "Songs."

- Of the song "You And Me Against The World," Helen says it is her "...second-most-requested song after "I Am Woman." I still receive mail from people who have lost a parent or child telling me that this was "their song." These letters always touch me."

HELEN REDDY

A promotional picture taken for the album.
A similar image appears on the back jacket of the album and includes
Helen and Jeff's son, Jordan.

Free and Easy
ST-11348

H E L E N   R E D D Y

Free and Easy

Track Listing:
Angie Baby / Raised On Rock / I've Been Wanting You So Long / You Have Lived / I'll Be Your Audience / Emotion / Free And Easy / Loneliness / Think I'll Write A Song / Showbiz

Production Information:
Produced by: Joe Wissert
Recorded at: Hollywood Sound, The Burbank Studios and Capitol Records, Los Angeles, CA
Engineers: Tom Perry / Bruce Botnick
Cover Illustration: Michael Bryan
Art Direction: Roy Kohara

Singles Released From This Album:
"Angie Baby" b/w "Think I'll Write A Song" - October 7, 1974 (peaked at # 1 in the US on the Hot 100 Singles chart and # 1 in Canada on the *RPM* chart)
"Emotion" b/w "I've Been Wanting You So Long" - January 20, 1974 (peaked at # 22 in the US on the Hot 100 Singles chart and # 25 in Canada on the *RPM* chart) Of Note: While the album track clocks at 4:10, the song "Emotion" was edited down to a 2:52 for the 7" single release.

Album Data:
Billboard Chart Debut: November 2, 1974
Highest Chart Position: 8
Billboard Chart: Top 200 Albums
Number of weeks on Chart: 28

Notes / Trivia:
- This album was released on LP, 8-Track and Cassette on October 22, 1974.
- The album was certified gold on December 18, 1974 for sales in excess of 500,000 copies.
- The Pointer Sisters provide background vocals on the track "Showbiz."
- Cashbox reviewed the album in the October 26, 1974 issue and said: "The mention of Helen's name immediately evokes memories of her many past #1 hits, but her new LP, like her previous ones, has a brand new smash, "Angie Baby" leading it magnificently out into the public eye. Helen's vocals are resplendent on every cut and once again she displays a flair and elan that equal star quality unequivocally. She sings the title track with an elegant carefree tone that matches Tom Jans' lyrics perfectly. Joe Wissert, Helen's producer, has done a great job highlighting the best that the talented songstress has to offer and it's easy to predict another big hit album here."
- This was Helen's 4th gold record for Capitol.

THE CAPITOL CAST FEATURES

Helen Reddy

Her latest album

Free and Easy

E-ST 11348
Also available on
cassette and cartridge.

Helen is performing in concert at New Theatre, Southport 25th April 2 concerts
Drury Lane Theatre, London 27th April 2 concerts
She is also recording a TV special as Glen Campbell's guest and being filmed
for her own BBC2 In Concert at Southport.

SEE HER ON
Top of the Pops
24 APRIL
Performing
HER NEW SINGLE
I Am Woman
CL 15815

Capitol

EMI

UK trade ad for the *Free and Easy* album.

No Way To Treat A Lady
ST-11418

Track Listing:
Ain't No Way To Treat A Lady / Bluebird / Don't Let It Mess Your Mind / Somewhere In The Night / You Don't Need A Reason / Ten To Eight / Birthday Song / You Know Me / Nothing Good Comes Easy / Long Time Looking

Production Information:
Produced by: Joe Wissert
Recorded at: Hollywood Sound, Hollywood, CA
Engineers: Tom Perry
Mastered by: Doug Sax and Mike Reese at The Mastering Lab, Los Angeles, CA
Cover Photography: Francesco Scavullo
Art Direction: Roy Kohara

Artist Management: Jeff Wald

Singles Released From This Album:
"Bluebird" b/w "You Don't Need A Reason" - June 1975 (peaked at # 35 in the US on the Hot 100 Singles chart and # 51 in Canada on the *RPM* chart)
"Ain't No Way To Treat A Lady" b/w "Bluebird" - August 1975 (peaked at # 8 in the US on the Hot 100 Singles chart and # 2 in Canada on the *RPM* chart)
"Somewhere In The Night" b/w "Ten To Eight" - November 17, 1975 (peaked at # 19 in the US on the Hot 100 Singles chart and # 27 in Canada on the *RPM* chart)

Album Data:
Billboard Chart Debut: July 12, 1975
Highest Chart Position: 11
Billboard Chart: Top 200 Albums
Number of weeks on Chart: 34

Notes / Trivia:
- This album was released on LP, 8-Track, Open Reel and Cassette June 10, 1975.
- The album was certified gold on January 19, 1976 for sales in excess of 500,000 copies.
- On August 23, 2005 the album was released on CD as a 2 on 1 disc along with the following album *Music, Music* but is now out of print.
- The title track also earned Reddy her final Grammy nomination, in the category of "Best Pop Vocal Performance, Female."
- Of "Somewhere In The Night" Helen said; "Barry Manilow also recorded this song but

graciously conceded that he thought my version was better," said Helen. "I don't think it's possible for anyone to make a bad recording of such a great tune."

Sheet music for Ain't No Way To Treat A Lady

Music, Music
ST-11547

Track Listing:
Music, Music / Gladiola / Mama / Hold Me In Your Dreams Tonight / Get Off Me Baby / I Can't Hear You No More / Ladychain / Music Is My Life / Nice To Be Around / You Make It So Easy

Production Information:
Produced by: Joe Wissert
Recorded at: Hollywood Sound, Hollywood, CA
Engineers: Tom Perry
Mastered by: Mike Reese at The Mastering Lab, Los Angeles, CA
Cover Photography: Jeff Dunas
Art Direction: Roy Kohara

Artist management: Jeff Wald

Musicians:
Drums: Jeff Porcaro / Harvey Mason
Piano: David Paich / Clarence McDonald / Mark Jordan / Larry Muhoberac
Bass Guitar: Reini Press / David Hungate
Guitar: Fred Tackett / Dean Parks / Ray Parker Jr.
Bass Guitar: Scotty Edwards
Percussion: Victor Feldman
Alto Flute: Tom Scott
Congas: Bobbye Hall
Horns: Gary Grant / Chuck Findley / Bob Findley / Steve Madiao / Jay Daversa / Don Menza / Tom Scott / Bill Perkins / Jay Migliori / Jack Nimitz / Dick "Slyde" Hyde / Lou McCreary / Earl Dumler
Background Vocalists: Carolyn Willis / Jim Gilstrap / Myrna Matthews / Oren Waters / Lisa Roberts / Nick DeCaro
Contractor: Frank DeCaro
Concertmaster: Harry Bluestone

Singles Released From This Album:
"I Can't Hear You No More" b/w "Music Is My Life" - July 26, 1976 (peaked at # 29 in the US on the Hot 100 Singles chart and # 36 in Canada on the *RPM* chart)
"Gladiola" b/w "You Make It So Easy" - December 17, 1976 (peaked at # 10 in the US on the Hot 100 Singles chart)

Album Data:
Billboard Chart Debut: August 14, 1976
Highest Chart Position: 16

Billboard Chart: Top 200 Albums
Number of weeks on Chart: 13

Notes / Trivia:

- This album was released on LP, 8-Track, Open Reel and Cassette Tape on July 6, 1976.
- Helen dedicates the album to then husband Jeff Wald.
- The album was certified gold on August 2, 1976 for sales in excess of 500,000 copies.
- *Music, Music* was cited in 1977 by Helen as a personal favorite from among her albums. It is also the author's favorite Helen Reddy album from song selection to graphic design.
- The flip side of "I Can't Hear You No More" ("Music Is My Life") eventually charted on the Hot 100 along with the A side as a "tag along." That showed that some radio stations were choosing to play the flip side of the original hit that charted.

Picture sleeve for "Music, Music" / "Ladychain" which was released as a single in Japan.

Ear Candy
SO-11640

Track Listing:
You're My World / One More Night / Long Distance Love / If It's Magic / Aquarius Miracle / Laissez Les Bontemps Rouler / The Happy Girls / Midnight Skies / Baby, I'm A Star / Thank You

Production Information:
Produced by: Kim Fowley & Earle Mankey
Recorded at: Brothers Studio, Santa Monica, CA
Recording and Mixing Engineer: Earle Mankey
Disc Mastering: Wally Traugott at Capitol Studios, Hollywood, CA
Cover Photography: Francesco Scavullo
Art Direction: Roy Kohara

Arrangements by: Rick Henn / Chris Darrow / Marc Peters / Kim Fowley / Earle Mankey

Musicians:
Arthur Amabe / Dorothy Ashby / Alfred Barr / Richard Bennett / Hal Blaine / H. Arthur Brown / Dennis Budimir / Denyse Buffum / David Carr / Stella Castellucci / Ronald Cooper / Chris Darrow / Richard Dickler / Assa Drori / Dave Duke / John Ethridge / Kim Fowley / Winterton Garvey / Nathan Gerschman / Harris Goldman / Gary Grant / Bob Henderson / Rick Henn / Mitch Holder / John Hornschuch / Jim Hughart / Dick Hyde / Dennis Karmazyn / Louis Kieveman / Bernard Leadon / Alan Lindgren / Leonard Malarsky / Earle Mankey / Gordon Marron / Mike Melvoin / Alex Neiman / Louis Newkirk / John Perez / Paul Poliynick / Jeff Porcaro / Mike Porcaro / Francis Reckard / Jerome Reisler / Emil Richards / Doug Rohen / Dale Rollice / Harry Roth / Henry Roth / Sheldon Sanov / Gene Sipriano / Bobby Shew / Jack Shulman / Marshall Sosson / Gloria Strassner / Robert Sushel / Ernie Tack / Dorothy Wade / Bill Watrous / John Wittenberg

Background Vocals:
Curt Becher / Joe Chemay / Laura Creamer / Pat Henderson / John Joyce / Stacey O'Brien / Gloria O'Brien / Myrna Matthews / Brent Nelson / Nigel Olsson / Helen Reddy on "Baby, I'm a Star" and "Thank You."

Singles Released From This Album:
"You're My World" b/w "Thank You" - April 4, 1977 (peaked at # 18 in the US on the Hot 100 Singles chart and # 13 in Canada on the *RPM* chart)
"The Happy Girls" b/w "Laissez Les Bontemps Rouler" September 1977 - (peaked at # 57 in the US on the Hot 100 Singles chart and # 65 in Canada on the *RPM* chart)

Album Data:
Billboard Chart Debut: May 21, 1977
Highest Chart Position: 75
Billboard Chart: Top 200 Albums
Number of weeks on Chart: 19

Notes / Trivia:
- This album was released on LP, 8-Track, Open Reel and Cassette Tape on April 25, 1977.
- Sessions for the album were conducted the first half of February 1977.
- Five tracks on the album were co-written by Helen Reddy.
- A rumored outtake from an Abbey Road Studios session by the Beatles from June 3, 1964 is said to include "You're My World." The tape is presumptively still in the Abbey Road vaults and has yet to be released.
- On February 23, 2010 the album was released on CD as a 2 on 1 disc along with the following album *We'll Sing in the Sunshine*.
- In the April 9, 1977 issue Cash Box says of "You're My World": "A definite change of pace from Ms. Reddy, who has delved into the past for a haunting song that was a hit for Cilla Black. Production by Kim Fowley keeps the sound on the appropriate pop music track, though there's still plenty of room for easy listening play. The right idea."
- "This album is dedicated to the public, who bought my first nine albums and have made this, my tenth album, possible."

The back side of the Italian picture sleeve for "You're My World" / "Thank you."

We'll Sing In The Sunshine
SO-11759

Track Listing:
Ready Or Not / All I Ever Need / Poor Little Fool / One After 909 / I'd Rather Be Alone / Lady Of The Night / Catch My Breath / We'll Sing In The Sunshine / Blue / If I Ever Had to Say Goodbye To You

Production Information:
Produced by: Kim Fowley / Nick DeCaro
Executive Producer: Charles Koppelman
Associate Producer: marc Peters
The Bottom Line: Helen Reddy
Recorded at: Larrabee Sound Studios / Sound Labs, Inc / A&M Studios in Los Angeles, CA, January and February 1978.
Engineers: Atmin Steiner / Taavi Moté / Steve Mitchell
Assistant Engineers: Sherry Klein / Linda Corbin
Mixed by:Earl Mallory at Hollywood Sound Studios, Hollywood, CA
Mastered by: John Golden
Cover Photography: Francesco Scavullo
Art Direction: Roy Kohara

Musicians:
Drums: Billy Thomas / Willie Ornelas / Ed Greene
Steel Guitar: Richard Bennett
Guitar: Doug Rohen / Jay Graydon / Mitch Holder / Richard Bennett / Thom Rotella / Dan Ferguson / Steve Lukather
Bass Guitar: David Hungate / Reini Press / Jim Hughart / Scott Edwards
Piano: Tom Hensley / Jai Winding
Keyboards: David Carr / Alan Lindgren / Eric Bikales
Percussion: Vince Charles / Gene Estes / Kim Fowley / Steve Forman
Harmonica ("We'll Sing in the Sunshine"): Ben Benay
Trumpet: Jay Daversa
Saxophone: Bud Shank
Synthesizers: Ian Underwood
Background Vocals: Laura Creamer / Mark Creamer / Denyce Deuschle / Barbara Cross / Nick Uhrig /Marc Piscitelli / Jim Gilstrap / Angela Winbush / Stephanie Spruill
Background Vocals on "We'll Sing in the Sunshine": Amy Boersma / Marcia Waldorf / Kate Hopkins / B. J. Emmons / Gale Kanter / David Carr / John Joyce / Mark Creamer / Jim McMains / Moose McMains

"We'll Sing In The Sunshine" b/w "I'd Rather be Alone" - March 27, 1978 (peaked at # 12 in the US on the Billboard Easy Listening Singles chart)

"Ready or Not" b/w "If I Ever Had To Say Goodbye To You" - July 1, 1978 (peaked at # 73 in the US on the Hot 100 Singles chart and # 70 in Canada on the *RPM* chart)

Album Data:

Billboard Chart Debut: —
Highest Chart Position: —
Billboard Chart: Top 200 Albums
Number of weeks on Chart: —

Notes / Trivia:

- This album was released on LP, 8-Track, Open Reel and and Cassette Tape on May 2, 1978
- In 2009 EMI Music Special Markets released *Rarities from the Capitol Vaults*, a 12-track CD of mostly previously unreleased Helen Reddy recordings. One of which is an alternate of the song "Blue." And three previously unreleased tracks from the 1978 album sessions. Those being: "Me and My Love," "Together" and "Rhythm Rhapsody."
- There was an advance March 1, 1978 release of the title cut single in Hawaii, with the anticipation a new single release would provoke some interest in Helen's high-profile Easter Sunday shows at the Sheraton Waikiki. It was also hoped that a sunny song might create an early breakout of the single in the tropical region. There was no such luck unfortunately.
- The title track was written by actress-singer Gale Garnett who had the first release with it in 1964 on RCA Records. Others who recorded the song are: Sonny & Cher for their 1967 album, *In Case You're in Love.* Dolly Parton for her album of covers, *The Great Pretender*.
- In the April 1, 1978 issue of Cash Box (and using the previous album's cover photo) The review for the "Feature Picks Singles" section it says of "We'll Sing In The Sunshine": "The production by Kim Fowley on this cover of the Gale Garnett tune is an impeccable blend of harmonica, guitar, string and horn work. The beat is gentle. Helen's voice is squeaky clean. Pop and MOR playlist material."
- In the May 13, 1978 issue Cash Box gave the album a review: "Grammy winner Helen Reddy's 11th Capitol LP presents a bright, yet tender package of love songs that reflect love's many moods. Included are the works of songwriters great and small, from Lennon-McCartney to unknowns, and even a song written for Reddy by ELO's Jeff Lynne, "Poor Little Fool." The title track, out as a single, fits Reddy's feminist image — strong but not strident. A tight, tasty MOR and pop offering."
- In the May 27, 1978 issue of Cash Box in the "Singles to Watch" section it says of "Ready or Not": "Strong phone action prompted Capitol to pull this flip - side of the first release, "We'll Sing In The Sunshine." A lavish string arrangement, steady beat, easy funk and sweeping chorus is the reason. Pop and MOR candidate."

Helen sang the album title track on *The Muppet Show* which aired on September 21, 1978

Reddy
SO-11949

Track Listing:
Trying To Get To You / Perfect Love Affair / The Magic Is Still There / Make Love To Me / Minute By Minute / Let Me Be Your Woman / You're So Good / Words Are Not Enough / Sing My Heart Out

Production Information:
Produced by: Frank Day
Associate producer: Bruce Sperling
Recorded and Mixed at: Conway Recording Studios, Hollywood, CA
Engineers: Buddy Brundo
Assistant Engineers: Cris Gordon / Phil Moores
Mastered by: Ken Perry at Capitol Studios, Hollywood, CA
Cover Photography: Claude Mougin
Art Direction: Roy Kohara

Musicians:
Drums: James Gadson / Ed Greene / Danny Seraphine / Chet McCracken
Percussion: Laudir de Oliveira
Keyboards: Teddy Randazzo / Pete Robinson / Jai Winding / Bill Cuomo / Robert Lamm
Guitar: Paul Jackson Jr. / Robert Bowles / Thom Rotella / Robert White / Bill Neale / Ira Newborn
Bass Guitar: Eddie Watkins, Jr. / Scott Edwards / Chuck Rainey / Leon Gaer
Sax Solo: Ernie Watts
Horn Section: Tower of Power / James Pankow / Lee Loughnane / Ernie Watts / Lee Loughnane / Steve Kupka / Greg Adams / Ricky Baptist / Steve Madio / Oscar Brashear / Jerry Hey / Gary Grant / Alan Kaplan / James Pankow / Charles Loper / Jack Redmond Lew McCreary / Emilio Castillo / Lenny Pickett / Mic Gillette / Bill Green / Terry Harrington
Background Vocals: Robert Lamm / Jon English / Dan Hamilton / Brenda Jones / Shirley Jones / Valorie Jones and The Sweet Inspirations

Arranged by: McKinley Jackson / James Pankow / Greg Adams / John Florez / D'Arneill Pershing / Frank Day

Artist Management: Jeff Wald

Singles Released From This Album:
"Make Love To Me" b/w "Trying To Get To You" - May 1979 (peaked at # 60 in the US on the Hot 100 Singles chart and # 57 in Canada on the *RPM* chart) (7' and 12" singles of this single released)
"Let Me Be Your Woman" b/w "More Than You Could Take"

Album Data:
Billboard Chart Debut: —
Highest Chart Position: —
Billboard Chart: Top 200 Albums
Number of weeks on Chart: —

Notes / Trivia:
- This album was released on LP, 8-Track and Cassette Tape on July 3, 1979
- "Make Love to Me" was featured on Helen's ABC-TV Special which aired May 22, 1979.
- In 2009 EMI Music Special Markets released *Rarities from the Capitol Vaults*, a 12-track CD of mostly previously unreleased Helen Reddy recordings. One of which was an unreleased track from this album titled "Exhaustion."
- The flip side to "Let Me Be Your Woman" was taken from Helen's 2nd LP "Helen Reddy" from 1971.

Capitol
REG. U.S. PAT. OFF.

MFD. BY CAPITOL RECORDS, INC., A SUBSIDIARY OF CAPITOL INDUSTRIES-EMI, INC., U.S.A.

℗1979 Capitol Records, Inc.

MONO

P-4712
PRO-9092

(from the forthcoming LP "LET ME BE YOUR WOMAN" SO-11949)

NOT FOR SALE

Trajor Music Co.- ASCAP

Intro.—:11
3:48

Produced by Frank Day
Associate Producer Bruce Sperling

• UNAUTHORIZED DUPLICATION IS A VIOLATION OF APPLICABLE LAWS. •

HELEN REDDY
MAKE LOVE TO ME
(Yellowstone-Voice-Tinsley)

ALL RIGHTS RESERVED.

Capitol MARCA REG.

Promo single for "Make Love to Me."
Notice the original album title as mentioned in the lower left of the single label.

Take What You Find
SOO-12068

Track Listing:
Take What You Find / Killer Barracuda / A Way With The Ladies / Love's Not The Question / Last Of The Lovers / The One I Sing My Love Songs To / Wizard In The Wind / All I Really Need Is You / Midnight Sunshine / That Plane

Production Information:
Produced by: Ron Haffkine
Recorded at: Muscle Shoals Sound Studio, Sheffield, AL, and Sound Lab, Nashville, TN
Engineers: Jim Cotton / Steve Melton
Assistant Engineers: Chuck Ainlay / David Cherry / Pat Holt / Joe Scaife / Mary Reth McLemore
Cover Photography: Kevin Horan
Art Direction: Roy Kohara
Design: Phil Shima
Arrangers: Shane Keister / Mike Lewis

Artist Management: Jeff Wald

Musicians:
Keyboards: Clayton Ivey / Randy McCormick
Percussion: Mickey Buckins
Guitar: Larry Byrom / Mac McAnally / Jimmy Johnson / Rod Smarr
Drums: Roger Hawkin
Bass: David Hood
Background Vocals: Sheri Kramer / Lisa Silver / Diane Tidwell
Stings: The Shelly Kurland Strings
Horns: The Nashville Horns

Singles Released From This Album:
"Take What You Find" b/w "Love's Not The Question"
"Killer Barracuda" b/w "A Way With The Ladies"

Album Data:
Billboard Chart Debut: —
Highest Chart Position: —
Billboard Chart: Top 200 Albums
Number of weeks on Chart: —

Notes / Trivia:

- This album was released on LP, 8-Track and Cassette Tape on June 9, 1980.
- The first ads for the album were in Billboard and Cash Box the week of June 1-7, 1980. Cash Box reviewed the album the week of June 8-14, 1980.
- In The June 14, 1980 issue of Cash Box the review read: "Reddy's showing of a little thigh on the cover of this LP makes a nice visual metaphor for the new sensual direction that her music has taken. Provocative songs like "Take What You Find" and "A Way With The Ladies" show that the Australian songstress is willing to widen her horizons. The rest of the LP is chocked full of the familiar ballads, uptempo A/C numbers and light country tunes that have made her a platinum selling artist. Top tracks are "Last Of The Lovers" and "Midnight Sunshine."
- Also in the same issue above, in the section of *Singles to Watch,* concerning the first single "Take What You Find" it reads: "Reddy continues to shift musical gears, this time into a mid-tempo rock-dance groove, utilizing a thick electronic piano and drum mix to create a liquid rhythm and some sharp lead guitar for bite. The result should please Top 40 and dance programmers alike."
- This was Helen's final album for Capitol after 10 years with the label. Unfortunately, despite the good reviews in many of the music magazines, like the previous three albums: *We'll Sing in the Sunshine, Live In London* and *Reddy* it failed to sell adequately enough to reach *Billboard* magazine's list of the "200 Top LP's & Tapes." It also became her first album that didn't have a single appearing on either the "Billboard Hot 100" or the magazine's "Easy Listening" chart.

Picture sleeve for "Take What You Find" as released in The Netherlands.

Play Me Out
MCA-5202

Track Listing:
Optimism Blues / Do It Like You Done It When You Meant It / I Can't Say Goodbye To You / Save Me /
You Don't Have To Say You Love Me / The Stars Fell On California / I Don't Know Why (I Love That
Guy) / When I Dream / Let's Just Stay Home Tonight / Play Me Out

Production Information:
Produced by: Joel Diamond
Recorded at: Devonshire Sound Studio, Los Angeles, CA
Engineers: Bill Halverson
Assistant Engineer: Russell Schmitt
Cover Photography: Douglas Kirkland
Art Direction: George Osaki
Graphics: Michael Kevin Lee
Arrangers / Conductors: Artie Butler / Gene Page / Charles Calello / Joel Diamond

Artist Management. Jeff Wald

Musicians:
Drums: John Guerin
Percussion: Gary Coleman
Guitar: Robben Ford / Thom Rotella / Waddy Wachtel / Timothy May
Bass Guitar: Larry Klein
Keyboards: John Barnes / Ron Fever
Conga & Bongos: Eddie "Bongo" Brown
Sax Solo ("Let's Just Stay Home Tonight"): Jim Horn
Sax Solo ("The Stars Fell on California"): Ernie Watts
Trumpet Solo ("Play Me Out"): Rick Baptist
Tambourine & Hand Claps ("Play Me Out"): Helen Reddy and Rhythm Section
Background Vocals: Joel Diamond / Denise Maynelli / Marti McCall / Myrna Matthews / Julia Waters
Tillman / Maxine Waters Willard / Clydene Jackson / Oren Waters / Luther Waters

Singles Released From This Album:
"I Can't Say Goodbye To You" b/w "Let's Just Stay Home Tonight" - (peaked at # 88 in the US on the
Hot 100 Singles chart, # 43 in Europe on the UK chart and # 16 in Ireland)
"The Stars Fell In California" b/w "When I Dream"

Album Data:
Billboard Chart Debut: —
Highest Chart Position: —
Billboard Chart: Top 200 Albums
Number of weeks on Chart: —

Notes / Trivia:
- This album was released on LP, 8-Track and Cassette Tape on April 28, 1981
- In the May 2, 1981 issue of Record World the review reads: "Helen Reddy is one of the most gifted and popular female vocalists in popular music. She has won virtually every award and performed in nearly every major venue around the world. She has also been honored with nine gold and three platinum albums. And she's now with MCA. "Play Me Out" is the latest chapter in this remarkable story that at one time included an incredible string of Top 10 hits. She's also been in Top 40, AOR and R&B charts at the same time, which shows the extent of her popularity with various audiences. "Play Me Out" features Helen's first MCA single entitled *I Can't Say Goodbye To You.*"

MCA RECORDS
103 267

The single for "I Can't Say Goodbye To You" from the Netherlands.

Imagination
MCA-5376

Track Listing:
Handsome Dudes / Don't Tell me Tonight / A Winner In Your Eyes / Let's Go Up / Imagination / Looks Like Love / The Way I Feel / Guess You Had To Be There / Yesterday Can't Hurt Me / Heartbeat

Production Information:
Produced by: Joe Wissart
Recorded & Mixed at: Hollywood Sound Recorders, Hollywood, CA
Recording & Mixing Engineers: Tom Perry / Ross Pallone
Mastered By Mike Reese at The Mastering Lab, Los Angeles, CA
Cover Photography: George Hurrell
Art Direction: Vartan
Graphics: Taki Ono
Artist Management: Michael Gardner Co.
Contractor: Frank DeCaro
Concertmaster: Harry Bluestone

Musicians:
Drums: Ricky Lawson / David L. Kemper / Vinnie Colaiuta / John Robinson
Piano: GSI / Yamaha / Fender Rhodes / Synthesizer / Wurlitzer Electric Piano: Robbie Buchanan
Bass: Nathan East / Neil Stubenhaus
Synth Bass: Nathan East
Guitar: Martin Walsh / Paul Jackson Jr.
Alto Sax solo: Lori B. Williams
Vibes: Kenny Watson
Timbales: Paulinho da Costa
Didgeridoo: Richard Walley
Steel Drums: Robert Greenidge
Strings: Sheldon Sanov / Reginald Hill / Marvin Limonick / Stanley Plummer / Sid Page / William Hymanson / Henry Ferber / Ronald Folsom / Vicki Sylvester / Denyse Buffum / Dan Neufeld / Armand Kaproff / Paula Hochhalter / Harry Bluestone
Horns: Larry Williams / Jerry Hey / Bill Reichenbach Jr. / Kim Hutchcroft / Gary Grant – horn
Background Vocals: Helen Reddy / Lori B. Williams / Arnold McCuller / David Lasley / Michael McDonald / Charlotte Crossley / Carmen Grillo / Jo Ann Harris

Singles Released From This Album:
"Don't Tell Me Tonight" b/w "Yesterday Can't Hurt Me"
"Imagination" b/w "The Way I Feel"
"Imagination" 12" single with extended version on side A and album version and side B.

Album Data:
Billboard Chart Debut: —
Highest Chart Position: —
Billboard Chart: Top 200 Albums
Number of weeks on Chart: —

Notes / Trivia:
- This album was released on LP, 8-Track and Cassette Tape on February 1, 1983.
- Songs recorded for the album, but unreleased: "You Pick Me Up" / Fallin' In Love For The Last Time This Time" recorded February 19, 1982 and "Daddy" recorded May 17, 1982. "Daddy" was replaced with "Guess You Had To Be There" during song revision prior to release.
- For the first single release from the album Cash Box said in its February 5 issue: "Helen Reddy steps out to a brisk dance beat on this first single from her new "Imagination" album. While the contemporary tempo — there's even use of electronic drumclaps — is a change from her earlier work, the self-assured vocal style remains."
- In the February 19 issue of Cash Box the review of the LP reads: "Strangely enough, this platter of soft pop ditties and MOR ballads is dedicated to the memory of "Joliet Jake" (John Belushi's Blues Brothers nom de plume). But while there are some moments when Reddy does get a little hard-edged and gutsy — most noticeably on the closing "Heartbeat" and the R&B-tinged dancer "The Way I Feel" — this is a package geared primarily towards Reddy's A/C fans. Horn and string arrangements on some tunes give additional oomph to the artist's self-confident vocals, while background harmonies feature white soulsters David Lasley and Michael McDonald. Prime picks for mellow pop programmers include Mann & Weil's "Handsome Dudes" and Dennis Lambert & Brian Potter's "Yesterday Can't Hurt Me.""
- This album, like the previous one, did not chart anywhere. Helen was subsequently dropped from MCA after its release. In Helen's 2006 autobiography, *The Woman I Am: A Memoir*, she wrote, "I was not surprised when I received a form letter from MCA's legal department telling me that I'd been dropped from the label."

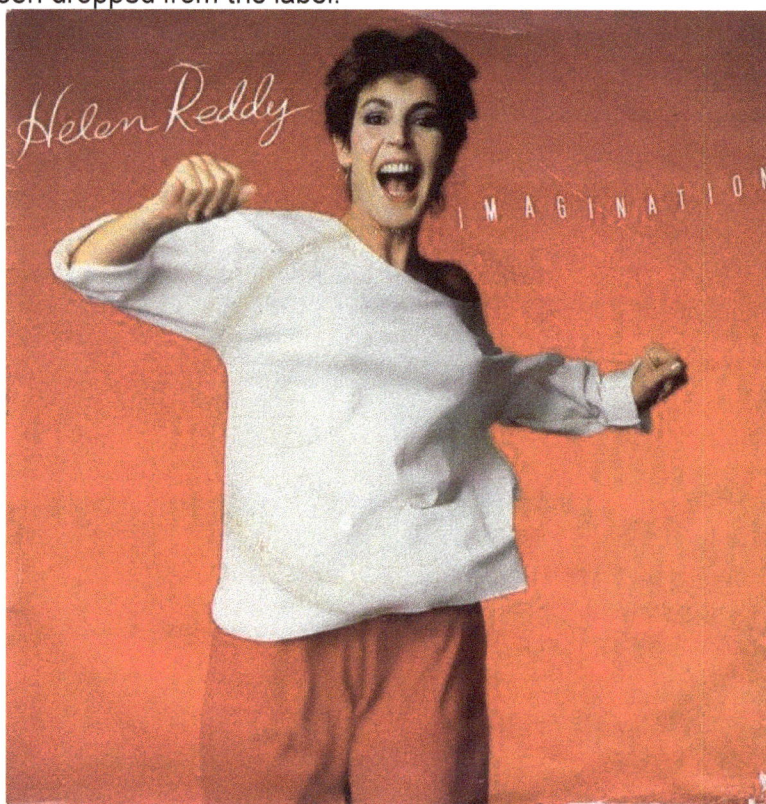

Picture sleeve for "Imagination" / "The Way I Feel" as released in Europe.

Feel So Young
HR-1

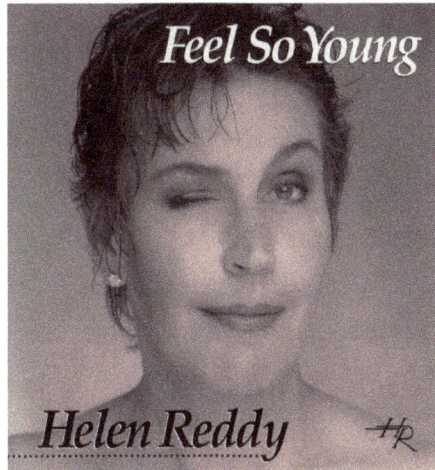

Track Listing:
Feel So Young / Ain't No Way To Treat A Lady / Let's Go Up / Angie baby / Here In My Arms / Looks Like Love / You And Me Against The World / Lost In The Shuffle / I Am Woman / That's All

Production Information:
Produced by: Dan Garcia & Milton Ruth
Executive Producer: Helen Reddy
Recorded & Mixed at: Groove Masters, Santa Monica, CA in August 1990
Engineer: Dan Garcia
Assistant Engineer: Paul Dieter
Mastered by: Doug Sax at The Mastering Lab, Hollywood, CA
Cover Photography: Jim Britt
Art Direction & Design: Garrett Burke

Musicians:
Lead Vocals: Helen Reddy
Drums: Milton Ruth
Piano: Wally Minko
Bass: Bill Breland
Guitar: Teresa Russell
Alto and Tenor Sax: Doug Norwine
Flugel Horn and Trumpet: Rick Baptist
Background Vocals: Bill Breland / Teresa Russell
Background Vocal solos: Jessica Williams

Notes / Trivia:
- This album was released on CD and Cassette Tape in November 1990
- This album is a collection of re-recorded material.
- This album was originally issued by Helen in the US, Japan and England on her own label but was licensed to at least ten other labels throughout Europe and Australia. Some of the reissues included these bonus tracks: "Leave Me Alone (Ruby Red Dress) / "I Don't Know How to Love Him" / "Delta Dawn. The re-issues went by various titles such as "Greatest and Latest," "The Collection" and "Classics." Each re-issues features different cover graphics.
- The original release used environmentally sensitive packaging as the insert stated. This used 90% less plastic and 70% less paper in a clear re-closable CD envelope.

Center Stage
VSD-5962

Track Listing:
Blow, Gabriel, Blow / I Still Believe In Love / A Boy Like You / The Writing's On The Wall / With Every Breath I Take / Knowing When To Leave / Love, Look Away / Surrender / You're Just In Love (Duet with Richard Hillman) / Tell Me It's Not True / Speak Low / My Friend / Fifty Percent / The Party's Over

Production Information:
Produced by: Bruce Kimmel
Recorded at: Westlake Audio, Los Angeles, CA
Engineers: Vincent Cirilli
Assistant Engineers: Michael Parnin / Markus Ulibarri
Mastered By: Joe Gastwirt at OceanView Digital Mastering, Los Angeles, California
Orchestrations and Music Preparation: Steven Orich
Arranger and Conductor: Ron Abel
"Tell Me It's Not True" arranger and orchestration: Joseph Baker
Assistant to the Producer: Esther Monk
Cover Photography: Kevin Merrill
Art Direction: Michael Caprio
Album coordinator: Brian Giorgi
Hair and Makeup Samantha Weaver
"Surrender" vocal group: Peyce Byron / Sabrina Cowans / Michele Mais / Brenda Silas Moore / Wayne Moore.

Singles Released From This Album:
"Surrender" (The Remix) b/w "Surrender" (Album Version) September 1998. This single was available on 12" vinyl and standard CD.

Notes / Trivia:
- This album was released on CD on September 22, 1998
- In the December 5, 1998 issue of *Billboard* the review reads: "Helen Reddy has had untold recording success. It's not that she has refashioned her vocal approach— it remains an affecting ballad voice. But it's employed in the interest here of classy, mostly rarely recorded ballads from the world of musical theater. That includes some choice rarities, among them Kurt Weill and Langston Hughes' touching "A Boy Like You" from "Street Scene," Rupert Holmes' "The Writing On The Wall" from "The Mystery Of Edwin Drood," Burt Bacharach and Hal David's "Knowing When To Leave" from "Promises, Promises" and Rodgers and Hammerstem's "Love, Look Away" from "Flower Drum Song." There is also comic relief in Irving Berlin's contrapuntal "You're Just In Love," with vocalist Richard Hillman. Reddy makes daring choices throughout this album and meets the challenge every time."

- "Surrender" is from The Broadway Musical "Sunset Blvd."

Both the 12" vinyl single and the CD release used this cover artwork of Helen with some rather beefy men.

The Best Christmas Ever
CD-1006

Track Listing:

The Best Christmas Ever / It's The Most Wonderful Time Of The Year / The Christmas Waltz / The Christmas Song / Sleigh Ride / Christmas Mem'ries / Deck The Halls / (Wishing You) An Old Fashioned Christmas / Have Yourself A Merry Little Christmas / Rudolph The Red-Nosed Reindeer / I'll Be Home For Christmas / Jingle Bells / We Wish You A Merry Christmas / The Christmas Of Your Life / There's No Christmas Like A Home Christmas / Christmas Auld Lang Syne

Notes / Trivia:

- This album was released on CD in 2000 by Helen Reddy, Inc through Select Media Concepts.
- Several different budget versions of this album were released with 10 songs, different title and re-designed cover artwork.

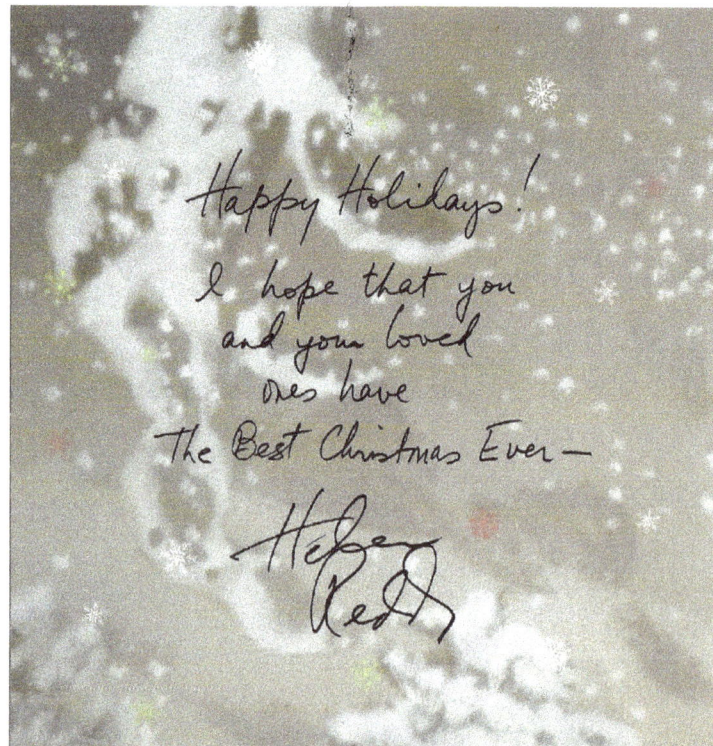

Happy Holidays!
I hope that you
and your loved
ones have
The Best Christmas Ever —

Helen
Reddy

The CD case interior

I Am Woman
CLO-2253

Track Listing:

I Am Woman / Angie Baby / You And Me Against The World / I Don't Know How To Love Him / That's All / Here In My Arms / Leave Me Alone (Ruby Red Dress) / Delta Dawn / Feel So Young / All You Need Is Love

Production Information:

Produced by: Dan Garcia / Milton Ruth / Sherman Heinig / Billy Sherwood

Recorded at: Jackson Browne's Private Studio, Los Angeles, CA (Side A Tracks 1-3, 5, Side B Tracks 1 & 4 in 1994) / Side A Track 4, Side B tracks 2-3 recorded in July 2002 in Los Angeles, CA / Side B Track 5 recorded in 2014.

Cover Photography: Barry Plummer

Notes / Trivia:

- This album was released on CD and vinyl LP on April 2, 2021. The information presented here is for the LP.
- The CD copy has four additional tracks, including a re-recording of "Ain't No Way To Treat A Lady."

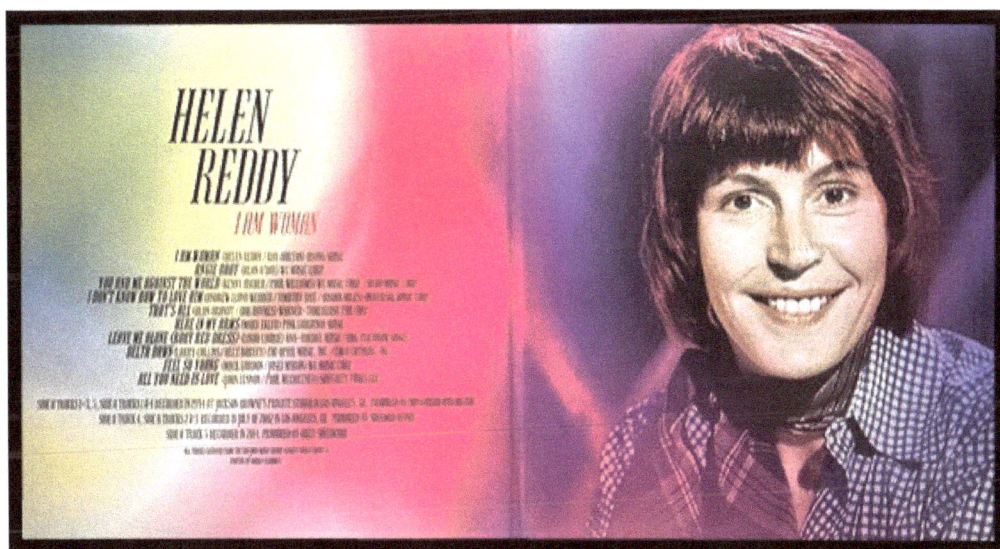

Interior of the gate fold jacket.

The Photo Gallery

→

STEREO ST-762
HELEN REDDY   I DON'T KNOW HOW TO LOVE HIM

Capitol.

It is very sobering to see the beautiful cover of Helen's first LP, shot in March 1971 and then to see how much the area the cover was shot at has changed and degraded. The cover was shot on Argyle Avenue in Los Angeles just a few blocks from the Capitol Records headquarters under the 101 Freeway overpass. Helen would have stood in line with the contraction joint to the left of the sign.

Google Earth
© 2021 Google

Helen in the 1960's

A Young, Beautiful Helen

THE CAPITOL CAST FEATURES

Helen Reddy

Her latest album

Free and Easy

E-ST 11348
Also available on
cassette and cartridge

Helen is performing in concert at New Theatre, Southport 25th April 2 concerts
Drury Lane Theatre, London 27th April 2 concerts
She is also recording a TV special as Glen Campbell's guest and being filmed
for her own BBC2 In Concert at Southport.

Capitol

SEE HER ON
Top of the Pops
24 APRIL

Performing

HER NEW SINGLE
I Am Woman
CL 15815

EMI

A promotional ad from the UK

Helen Reddy

Program price $2.00

A concert program from around 1972.
Photo taken at the same session for the LP cover *I Am Woman*.

Helen with Anne Murray during the Capitol Recording Studio sessions when Anne was working with Glen Campbell on their duet album in 1971. Helen was also in the process of recording her second album at this time in the adjacent studio.

Helen as "Sister Ruth" in Airport 1975

Capitol Records
Congratulates
Helen Reddy
#1 New Female Vocalist
(Singles)
1971
Annual Cash Box Poll

Capitol.

Management, De Blasio & Wald Inc.
Producer, Larry Marks

The staff and friends at
Irving Music
wish to congratulate
Helen Reddy
on her number 1 single
"I Am Woman"

Irving Music (BMI)/Almo Music (ASCAP)/ The Rondor Group
PUBLISHERS OF FINE MUSIC

NBC COLOR TELEVISION

<u>EXCLUSIVE TO YOU IN YOUR AREA</u>

SUMMER SHOW -- Helen Reddy plays hostess to a variety of
performers including Joan Rivers and Anne Murray on NBC-
TV's "Flip Wilson Presents The Helen Reddy Show," <u>Thurs-
day, July 19</u> (8-9 p.m. PT) in color.

**A Gold album award for the 1974 LP "Love Song For Jeffrey"
that had been presented to Jeff Wald.**

As our contribution
to the U.N. International
Women's Year
Stewart Macpherson's
STETSON
PRODUCTIONS
proudly present
for the first time
in New Zealand,
live on stage

helen Reddy

with her own musicians, supported by singer/songwriter **PETER ALLEN**

Playing
Auckland Town Hall   October 6th, 6 & 8.30 pm
Wellington Town Hall   October 7th, 6 & 8.30 pm
Christchurch Town Hall   October 9th, 6 & 8.30 pm

See Helen on Television One
Hear Helen on Radio Hauraki, Radio Windy, Radio Avon

A happy Helen doing what she loves to do — entertain!

An industry ad for Helen's concert at Lake Tahoe in 1978

A Gold single award for "Leave Me Alone (Ruby Red Dress)"

Full frame transparency showing Helen in 1977

Above, below and following pages Helen during rehearsals for "Pete's Dragon" in 1976

Another rehearsal shot during "Pete's Dragon."

Above rehearsal for "Pete's Dragon"

Below a promotional photo used for the film

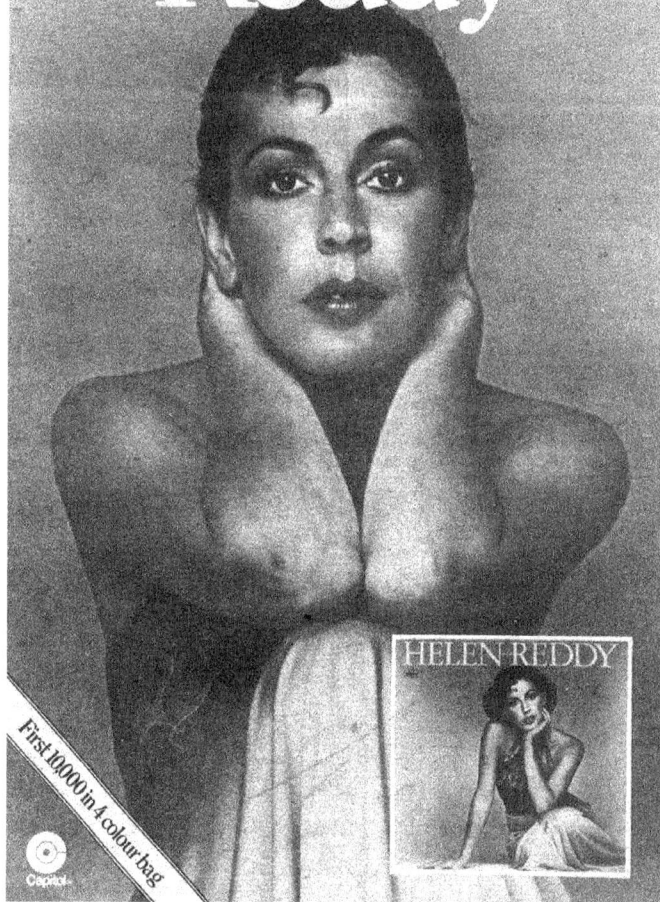

A rather hazy ad for "Long Distance Love."
Long distance love can be hazy!

Many of Helen's albums were issued in the open reel format.

Below a UK ad for Helen's first two albums.

This page and following page: Trade ads for the 1978 LP
"We'll Sing In The Sunshine."

Helen and guests Elliot Gould and Jane Fonda from Helen's May 22, 1979 TV Special on ABC-TV.

LOOK NO FARTHER THAN

HELEN REDDY!

TAKE
WHAT YOU
SOO-12068 FIND
her sparkling
new studio
album

Features
the new hit
single
"Take
What You
Find" 4867

Management
Jeff Wald

Capitol

Available On
Capitol Records
& Cassettes

Producer and
Musical Director:
Ron Haffkine

International
Promotion Coordinator
Randy Miller

A 1980 trade ad for the LP "Take What You Find." This was Helen's final album for Capitol.

Helen with husband, Jeff Wald in 1979. Jeff gives the finger to the always harassing and ever present paparazzi. Seems Jeff is not happy to be Papped!

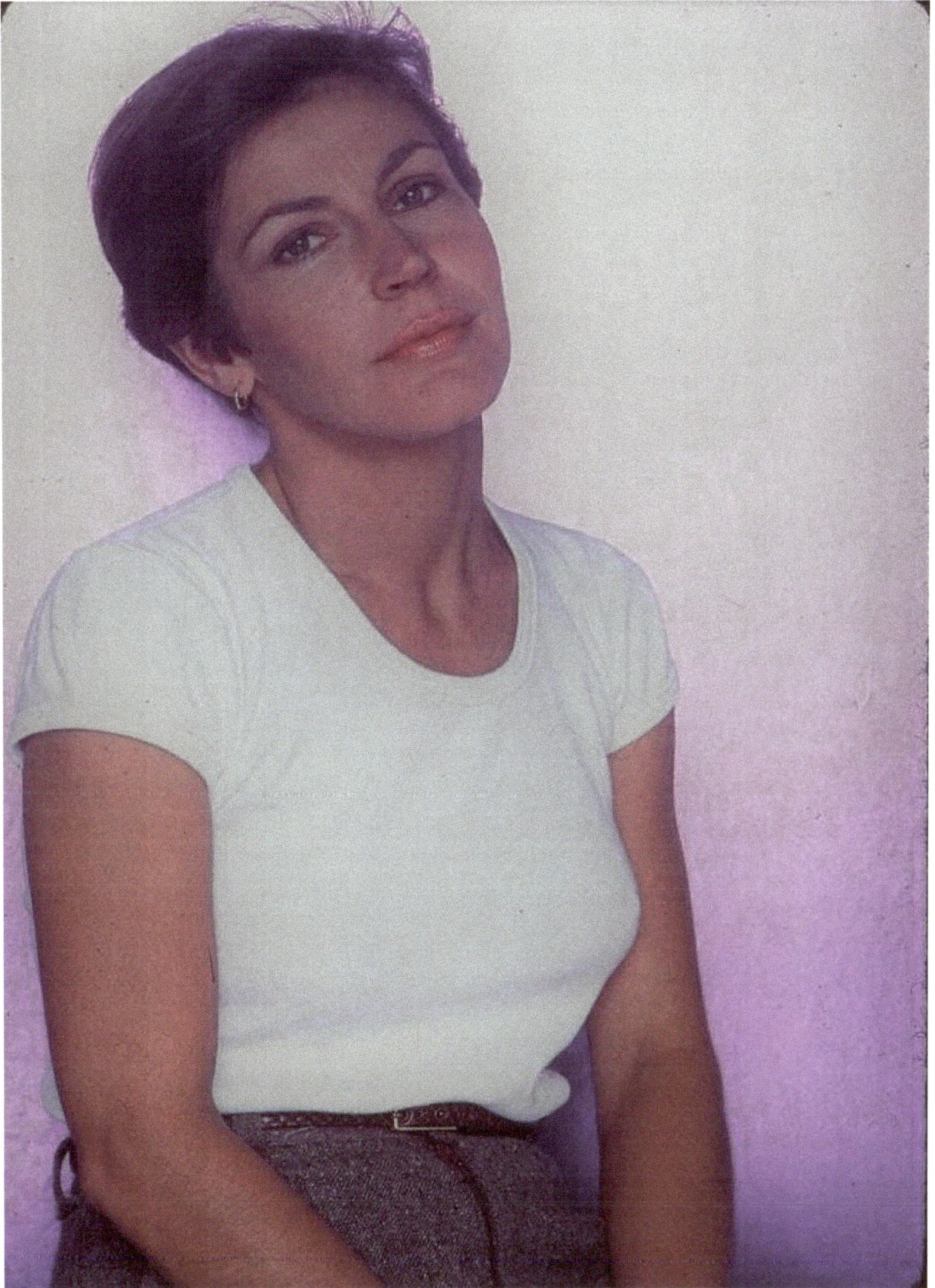

A pensive Helen poses for the camera in 1979

Luminous Helen in 1976

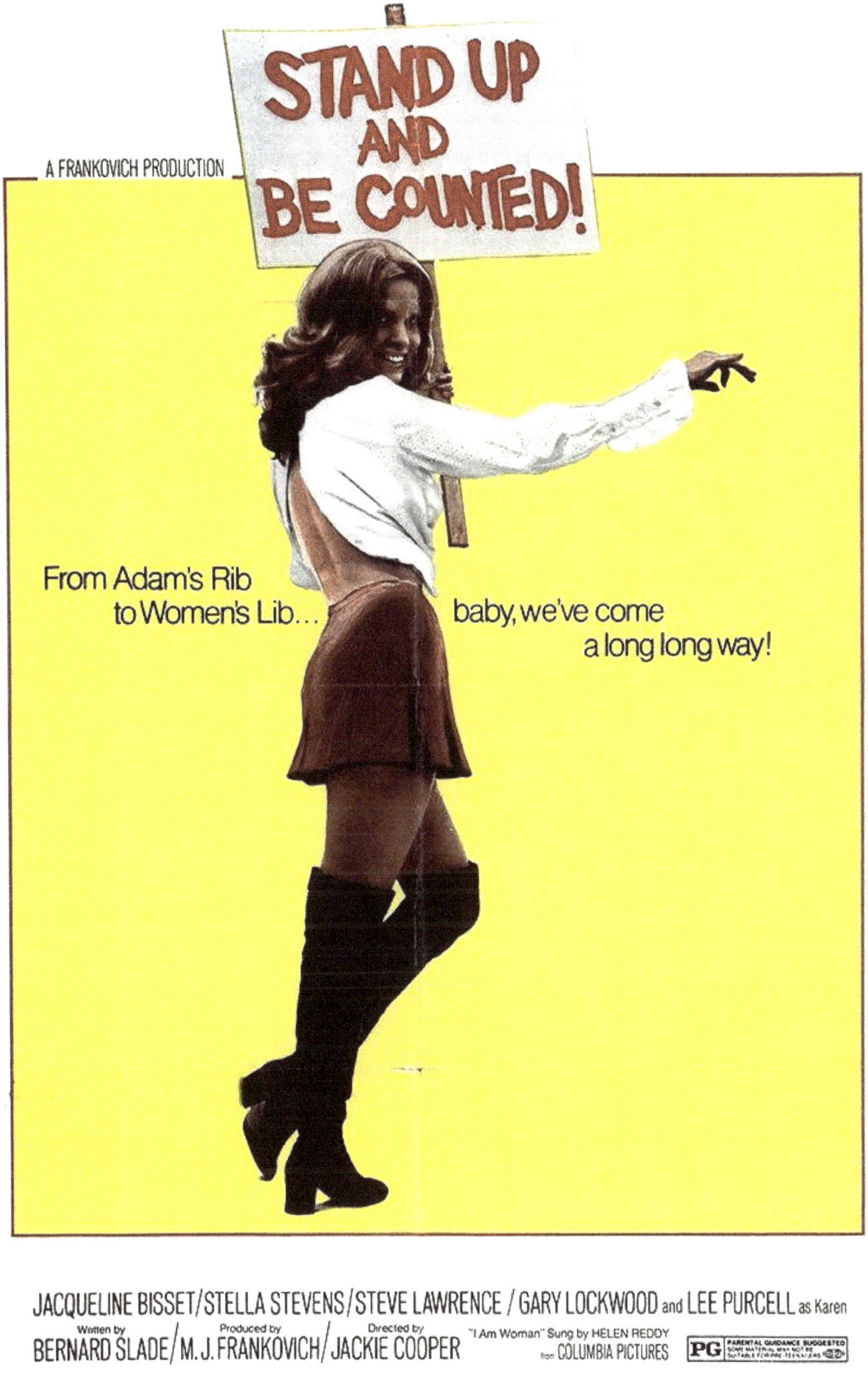

The poster for the film that featured "I Am Woman."

A trade ad for the 1974 single "Keep On Singing."

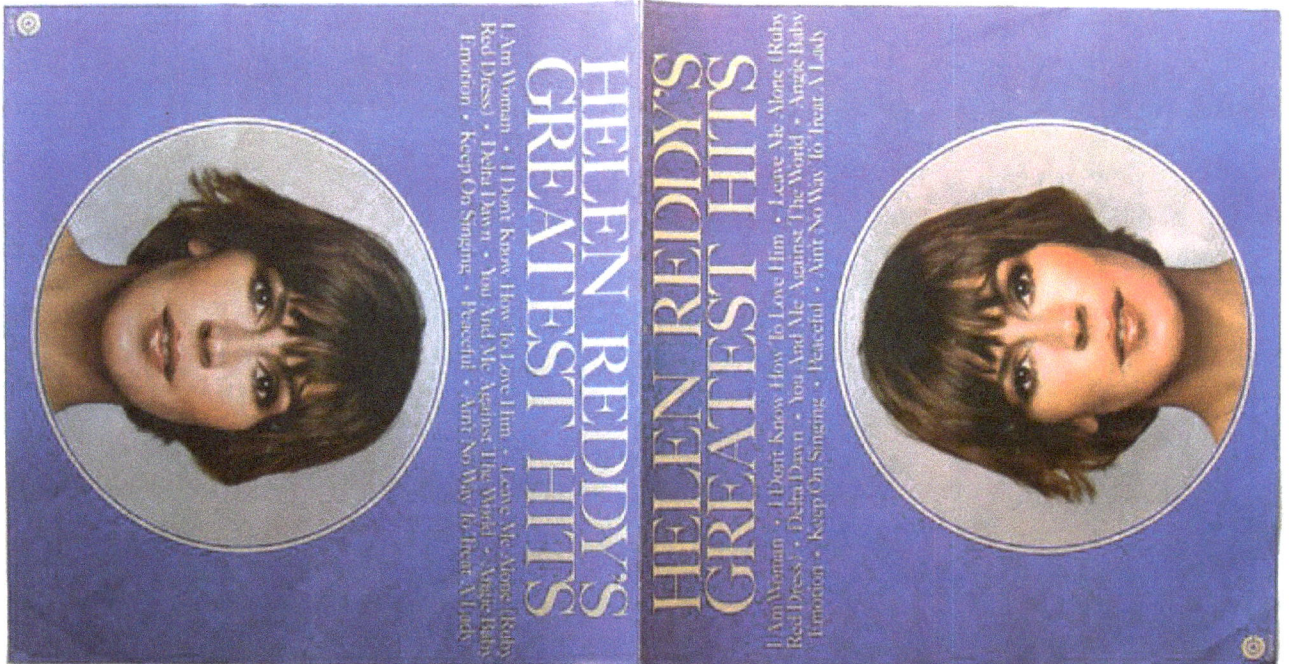

A "clothes hanger" type ad. Record stores hung these types of promo ads on wires that stretched the width or length of the store. The cover art could be seen from either side.

**A sophisticated Helen
in the 1980's**

The single for "I Don't Know How To Love Him" / "I Believe In Music" from Japan.

Helen on an episode of *Diagnosis Murder* from Season Seven. The title is "Swan Song" and Helen played a woman who is an international singer and is developing dementia. The episode aired on May 4, 2000.

KGW RADIO & NORTHWEST RELEASING PRESENT
HELEN REDDY
THE POINTER SISTERS
AUDITORIUM
THURS., DEC. 6
7:00 & 10:00 P.M.
Tickets on sale at Lipman's, Stevens & Sons, Lincoln Savings, Everybody's Records, and Auditorium
Washington Poster Co.

This has long been a favorite photo. Helen was so proud of her book and with good reason. The book is amazing. Helen told me that the cover photograph was her all-time favorite photograph of herself, that was why it was chosen. The uncropped photograph is also on the back jacket of her 1981 album "Play Me Out." It was photographed by Doug Kirkland.

WALT DISNEY PRODUCTIONS presents
"PETE'S DRAGON"
Starring: HELEN REDDY, JIM DALE, MICKEY ROONEY, RED BUTTONS
and SHELLEY WINTERS
Introducing: SEAN MARSHALL as PETE
Technicolor® Released by: Buena Vista Distribution Co., Inc.

Helen with handsome Cal Bartlett in 1977's Pete's Dragon.

Helen around 1972. To me this photo shows the simple, true beauty that she possessed. Helen didn't need to expose skin or wear tons of makeup to show that she was indeed an *extremely* talented singer / songwriter.
Her talent spoke for itself!

Helen at work in the recording studio in 1976 overdubbing vocals for "Candle on the Water."

Helen with the album of the week in 1974!

The Helen Reddy Album Discography

I DON'T KNOW HOW TO LOVE HIM • Helen Reddy #ST-762/Released May 1971

CRAZY LOVE • Van Morrison * Warner Bros. Music/Van-Jan Music/ASCAP 3:16
HOW CAN I BE SURE • F. Cavaliere–F. Brigati * Slacsar Music Co., Ltd./BMI 2:50
OUR HOUSE • Graham Nash * Giving Room Music/BMI 2:58
I AM WOMAN • H. Reddy–R. Burton * Buggerlugs Music/Inner Sense Music, Inc./BMI 2:15
L. A. BREAKDOWN • Larry Marks * La Brea Music/ASCAP 3:38

Side 1

A SONG FOR YOU • Leon Russell * Skyhill Publishing Co., Inc./BMI 3:03
DON'T MAKE PROMISES • Tim Hardin * Faithful Virtue Music Co., Inc./BMI 3:02
I BELIEVE IN MUSIC • Mac Davis * Songpainter Music, Inc./BMI 3:14
BEST FRIEND • H. Reddy–R. Burton * Buggerlugs Music/Inner Sense Music, Inc./BMI 2:17
I DON'T KNOW HOW TO LOVE HIM (from the Rock Opera "Jesus Christ, Superstar") •
A. L. Webber–T. Rice * Leeds Music Corporation/ASCAP 3:15

Side 2

PRODUCED BY: LARRY MARKS

HELEN REDDY • Helen Reddy #ST-857/Released November 1971

TIME • Paul Parrish * Kittyhawk Music/ASCAP 3:37
HOW • John Lennon * Maclen Music, Inc./BMI 3:10
COME ON JOHN • David Blue * Good Friends Music/BMI/ASCAP 4:20
SUMMER OF '71 • H. Reddy–J. Conrad * Irving Music Inc./Buggerlugs Music Co./BMI 2:28
I DON'T REMEMBER MY CHILDHOOD • Leon Russell * Skyhill Publishing Co., Inc./BMI 3:30

Side 1

NO SAD SONG • C. King–T. Stern * Screen Gems-Columbia Music, Inc./BMI 3:09
I THINK IT'S GOING TO RAIN TODAY • Randy Newman * January Music Corp./BMI 2:16
TULSA TURNAROUND • A. Harvey–L. Collins * Unart Music Corporation/BMI 3:32
MORE THAN YOU COULD TAKE • Helen Reddy * Buggerlugs Music Co./BMI 2:40
NEW YEAR'S RESOLUTION • Donovan Leitch * Donovan Music Ltd./BMI 3:37

Side 2

PRODUCED BY: LARRY MARKS

I AM WOMAN • Helen Reddy #ST-11068/Released November 1972*

PEACEFUL • Kenny Rankin * Four Score Music Corp./BMI 2:50
I AM WOMAN • H. Reddy–R. Burton * Buggerlugs Music Co./BMI 3:24
THIS MASQUERADE • Leon Russell * Skyhill Publishing Co., Inc./BMI 3:35
I DIDN'T MEAN TO LOVE YOU • A. Butler–K. Philipp * Hands Together Music/BMI 4:00
WHERE IS MY FRIEND • B. Scott–D. Meehan * Church Lane Music Inc./ASCAP 3:10

Side 1

AND I LOVE YOU SO • Don McLean * Mayday Music Inc./Yahweh Tunes, Inc./BMI 4:00
WHAT WOULD THEY SAY • Paul Williams * Almo Music Corp./Ampco Music, Inc./ASCAP 2:45
WHERE IS THE LOVE • R. MacDonald–W. Salter * Antisia Music Inc./BMI 3:01
HIT THE ROAD, JACK • P. Mayfield * Tangerine Music Corp./BMI 2:18
THE LAST BLUES SONG • B. Mann–C. Weil * Screen Gems-Columbia Music, Inc./Summerhill Songs, Inc./BMI 2:41

Side 2

PRODUCED BY: TOM CATALANO

LONG HARD CLIMB • Helen Reddy #SMAS-11213/Released August 1973*

LEAVE ME ALONE (Ruby Red Dress) • Linda Laurie * Anne-Rachel Music Corporation/ASCAP 3:26
LOVIN' YOU • John Sebastian * The Hudson Bay Music Co./BMI 2:49
A BIT O.K. • C. Sager–P. Allen * Valando Music, Inc./Sunbeam Music, Inc./ASCAP/BMI 2:07
DON'T MESS WITH A WOMAN • P. Moan–R. Curtis–M. Curtis * Catpatch Music/ASCAP 3:04
DELTA DAWN • A. Harvey–L. Collins *, United Artists Music Co. Inc./Big Ax Music/ASCAP 3:08

Side 1

THE WEST WIND CIRCUS • Adam Miller * Every Little Tune Inc./ASCAP 4:25
IF WE COULD STILL BE FRIENDS • Paul Williams * Almo Music Corp./ASCAP 2:17
LONG HARD CLIMB • Ron Davies * Irving Music, Inc./BMI 2:59
UNTIL IT'S TIME FOR YOU TO GO • Buffy Sainte-Marie * Gypsy Boy Music, Inc./ASCAP 2:17
THE OLD FASHIONED WAY • G. Garvarentz–A. Kasha–J. Hirschhorn * Chappell & Co., Inc./ASCAP 2:56

Side 2

PRODUCED BY: TOM CATALANO

LOVE SONG FOR JEFFREY • Helen Reddy #SO-11284/Released March 1974*

THAT OLD AMERICAN DREAM • M. Hazelwood–A. Hammond * April Music, Inc./Landers-Roberts Music Inc./ASCAP 2:27
YOU'RE MY HOME • Billy Joel * Blackwood Music, Inc./Tinker Street Tunes Co./BMI 2:59
SONGS • B. Mann–C. Weil * Screen Gems-Columbia Music, Inc./Summerhill Songs, Inc./BMI 3.55
I GOT A NAME • N. Gimbel–C. Fox * Fox Fanfare Music, Inc./BMI 3:32
KEEP ON SINGING • D. Janssen–B. Hart * Pocket Full Of Tunes, Inc./BMI 3:03

Side 1

YOU AND ME AGAINST THE WORLD • P. Williams–P. Ascher * Almo Music Corp./ASCAP 3:08
AH, MY SISTER • C. B. Sager–P. Allen * The Music Of The Times Publishing Corp. (Valando Music Division)/ASCAP 3:26
PRETTY, PRETTY • P. Allen–H. Hackady * The Music Of The Times Publishing Corp. (Valando Music Division)/ASCAP 3:26
LOVE SONG FOR JEFFREY • H. Reddy–P. Allen * Irving Music, Inc./Buggerlugs Music Co./Woolnough Music/BMI 2:40
STELLA BY STARLIGHT • N. Washington–V. Young * Famous Music Corp./ASCAP 3:50

Side 2

PRODUCED BY: TOM CATALANO

FREE AND EASY • Helen Reddy #ST-11348/Released October 1974*

ANGIE BABY • Alan O'Day * WB Music Corp./ASCAP 3:29
RAISED ON ROCK • Mark James * Screen Gems-Columbia Music, Inc./Sweet Glory Music, Inc./BMI 3:12
I'VE BEEN WANTING YOU SO LONG • P. Allen–J. Barry * Irving Music, Inc./Woolnough Music/Broadside Music/BMI 3:40
YOU HAVE LIVED • Don McLean * Unart Music Corporation/Yahweh Tunes, Inc./BMI 3:48
I'LL BE YOUR AUDIENCE • B. Hobbs–L. Anderson * Fairfield Music Corporation/Bad Boy Music/Harmony And Grits Music/BMI 3:19

Side 1

EMOTION • Lyrics by Dahlstrom Music by V. Sanson * WB Music Corp./ASCAP 4:10
FREE AND EASY • Tom Jans * Almo Music Corp./ASCAP 2:46
LONELINESS • P. Williams–K. Ascher * Twentieth Century Music Corp./Hobbitron Enterprises/Ashken Music Co./ASCAP 3:30
THINK I'LL WRITE A SONG • Lyrics by H. Reddy – Music by P. Allen/Irving Music, Inc./Buggerlugs Music Co./Woolnough Music/BMI 2:22
SHOWBIZ • Dennis Tracy * Almo Music Corp./ASCAP 3:04

Side 2

PRODUCED BY: JOE WISSERT

NO WAY TO TREAT A LADY • Helen Reddy #ST-11418/Released June 1975

AIN'T NO WAY TO TREAT A LADY • Words and Music by Harriet Schock * Colgems Music Corporation/ASCAP 3:26
BLUEBIRD • Leon Russell * Skyhill Publishing Co., Inc./BMI 2:46
DON'T LET IT MESS YOUR MIND • Neil Sedaka–Phil Cody * Don Kirshner Music, Inc./Kirshner Songs, Inc./BMI/ASCAP 2:42
SOMEWHERE IN THE NIGHT • Richard Kerr–Will Jennings * Irving Music, Inc./BMI/Rondor Music (London) Ltd. (Controlled in the United States & Canada by Almo Music Corp. – ASCAP) 3:31
YOU DON'T NEED A REASON • Alex Harvey * United Artists Music Co., Inc./Big Ax Music/ASCAP 2:59

Side 1

TEN TO EIGHT • David Castle * Unart Music Corporation/BMI 3:39
BIRTHDAY SONG • Don McLean * Yahweh Tunes, Inc./BMI 3:16
YOU KNOW ME • Paul Williams–Kenny Ascher * Almo Music Corp./ASCAP 2:44
NOTHING GOOD COMES EASY • Music by Barry Mann–Words: Cynthia Weil * Screen Gems-Columbia Music, Inc./Summerhill Songs Inc./BMI 3:15
(All administrative rights for the entire world controlled by Screen Gems-Columbia Music, Inc.)
LONG TIME LOOKING • Peter Allen–Carole Bayer Sager * Irving Music, Inc./Woolnough Music/The New York Times Music Corporation/BMI 2:46

Side 2

PRODUCED BY: JOE WISSERT

*asterisk indicates RIAA Certified Gold Records

An ad from Cashbox magazine Summer 1975. *After year denotes gold status.

REDDY

Helen finishes off the Seventies as she began it...
With a smash-hit album — REDDY SO-11949
Includes the hot disco single

"Make Love To Me" 4573
the perfect invitation.

Produced by FRANK DAY
Associate Producer:
BRUCE SPERLING for
Jeff Wald Productions., Inc.
Management: JEFF WALD

With Marie and Donny Osmond in early 1976. When asked Helen told me she loved these two! Below: Helen appears all week on The John Davidson Show starting December 8, 1980.

Get Reddy For Musical Magic!

NOW 90 MINUTES

All this week **Helen Reddy** teams up with John for a great musical time.

The JOHN DAVIDSON Show

All This Week

4 PM KPIX 5

Helen with good friend and fellow Aussie, Olivia Newton-John

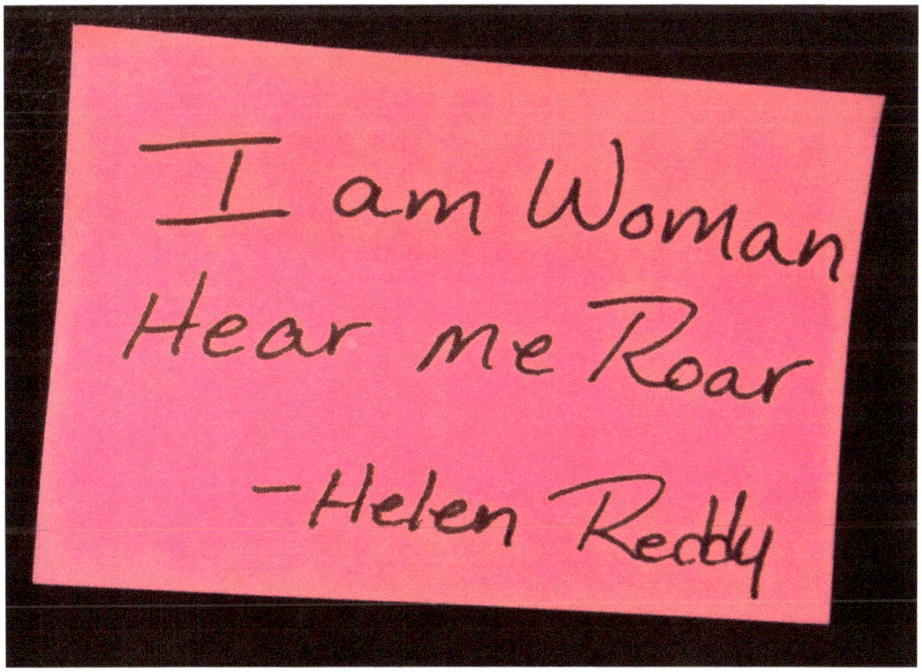

I am Woman
Hear me Roar

— Helen Reddy

A pretty special Post-It Note!

Above, Helen with Barbra Streisand. Each adored the other. 1979
Helen with former husband Milton Ruth. Milton was always nice to me when I saw him.

A unique, one-of-a-kind clock made
from an LP and cut with a laser.

Early in her U.S. career during an interview at home. Unknown publication.

QUAD 8

VAN MORRISON &
HELEN REDDY

PROGRAM I
I Am Woman
(Helen Reddy)
Blue Money
(Van Morrison)
Crazy Love (Helen Reddy)
Believe In Music
(Helen Reddy)
I Don't Know How To Love
Him (Helen Reddy)
Tulsa Turn Around
(Helen Reddy)

PROGRAM II
Domino (Van Morrison)
Brown Eyed Girl
(Van Morrison)
When That Evening Sun
Goes Down (Van Morri
No Sad Song (Helen Redd
Tupelo Honey
(Van Morrison)

VAN MORRISON
HELEN REDDY

PROGRAM I
I Am Woman (H. Reddy)
Blue Money (Van Morrison)
Tulsa Turn Around
(Helen Reddy)

PROGRAM II
Domino (Van Morrison)
Crazy Love (Helen Reddy)
Brown Eyed Girl
(Van Morrison)

PROGRAM III
No Sad Song (H. Reddy)
When That Evening Sun
Goes Down (V. Morrison)
I Don't Know How To Love
Him (Helen Reddy)

PROGRAM IV
I Believe In Music
(Helen Reddy)
Tupelo Honey
(Van Morrison)

Every popular artist has been bootlegged and Helen is no different.
Here are a few bootlegged 8 track tapes. One labeled as Quad.
Odd paring with Van Morrison who was on Warner Brothers Records.
Van Morison, however, did write Helen's hit "Crazy Love" which peaked at # 8 on 9/10/1971.

STEVE WOLF & JIM RISSMILLER
★★★★★★ present ★★★★★★
CARPENTERS/HELEN REDDY
★★★★★★★★★★★★★★★★★★
CONVENTION CENTER ARENA
MAY **29** 1976 Fresno, Calif.
SATURDAY
8:00 P.M.
TAX INCLUDED

BALCONY SEC 5 ROW N SEAT 3
MAY 29, 1976
ADMIT ONE ON ABOVE DATE ONLY
NO REFUND PRICE NO EXCHANGE
$6-50
SEC 5 ROW N SEAT 3 BALCONY

Back when money was worth more and music was actually good!

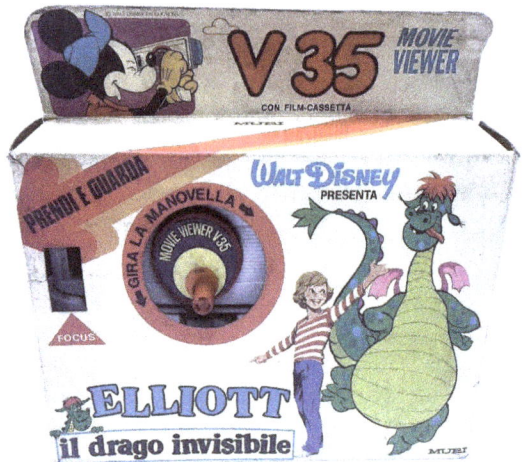

Some collectible items from Disney's 1977 film "Pete's Dragon."

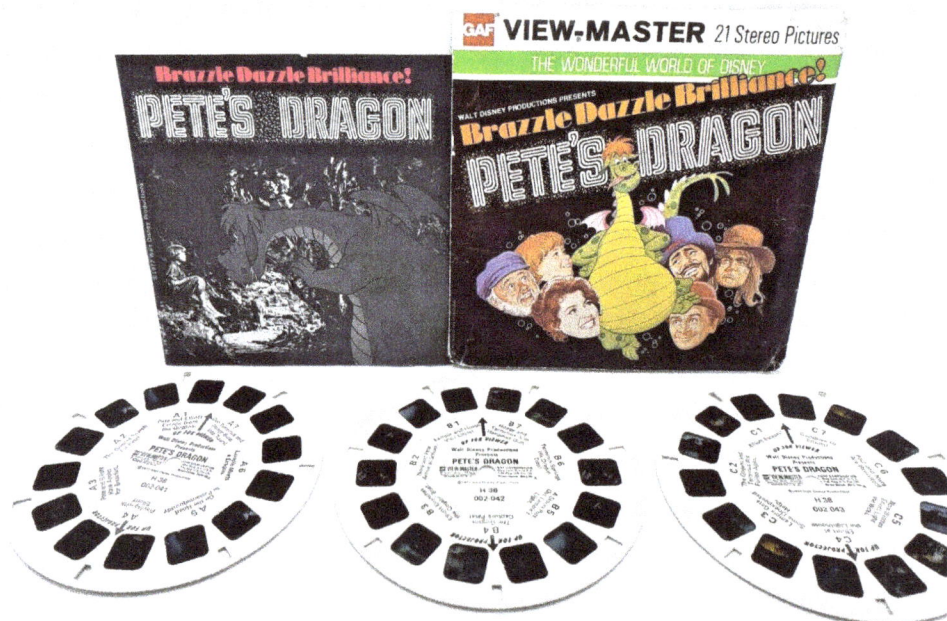

HELEN REDDY AND FRANK SINATRA...

HELEN REDDY LIVE IN LONDON

THE RARE SINATRA

...DYNAMITE!

Yes, I know she did.

HELEN REDDY
HIS GREATEST HITS

光美唱片
KONG MEI RECORD CO. LTD.
⇔STEREO⇔
KM-2001

排行之星
「海倫瑞蒂」
最佳專集之精華

A real oddity in my collection. I know it was the 1970's, but really.... did
Helen look like a man here?! I was always going to show this album to
Helen, but never got the nerve. She would have likely laughed.
Piracy at its worst!

Sheet Music & Songbooks

$\longrightarrow$

Helen has had *many* music folios and songbooks issued.
Here is just a small sampling!

angie baby

Words and Music by ALAN O'DAY

WARNER BROS. PUBLICATIONS INC.
75 Rockefeller Plaza / New York, N.Y. 10019

Recorded by HELEN REDDY on CAPITOL Records

$1.50
in U.S.A.

PEACEFUL

Words and Music by KEN RANKIN

Recorded by

HELEN REDDY

on CAPITOL Records

FOUR SCORE MUSIC CORP.

Charles Hansen
EDUCATIONAL MUSIC & books
0 Broadway / New York, New York 10023

1023ISM

I Didn't Mean To Love You

Lyric by KAREN PHILIPP

Music by ARTIE BUTLER

Recorded by HELEN REDDY on CAPITOL RECORDS

HANDS TOGETHER MUSIC $1.50

exclusive distributor
SCREEN GEMS-COLUMBIA PUBLICATIONS
a division of
COLUMBIA PICTURES INDUSTRIES, INC.
6744 N.E. 4th Avenue, Miami, Fla. 33138

Gladiola

Words and Music by ALAN GORDON

Recorded by HELEN REDDY on CAPITOL Records

KOPPELMAN-BANDIER MUSIC
New York, New York

$1.50

Distributed by
big3

BRADLEY
easy piano series

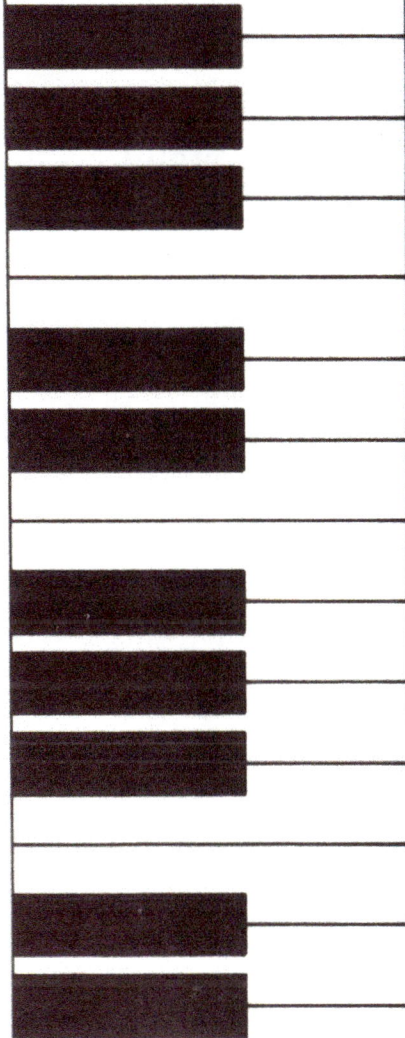

3734BP2

BLUEBIRD

Words and Music by LEON RUSSELL

Arranged by RICHARD BRADLEY

Recorded by HELEN REDDY on CAPITOL RECORDS

SKYHILL PUBLISHING CO., INC.

exclusive distributor
SCREEN GEMS-COLUMBIA PUBLICATIONS
a division of
COLUMBIA PICTURES INDUSTRIES, INC.
16333 N.W. 54th Avenue, Hialeah, Florida 33014

$1.00

LEAVE ME ALONE
(Ruby Red Dress)

Words and Music by LINDA LAURIE

Recorded by HELEN REDDY on CAPITOL Records

THE ABERBACH GROUP
Sole Selling Agent:
Hill and Range Songs, Inc.

1.25

Distributed by

THE HAPPY GIRLS

Words and Music by Helen Reddy, Kim Fowley, Earle Mankey and Rick Henn

Recorded by HELEN REDDY on Capitol Records

CRAZY LOVE

Words and Music by
VAN MORRISON

Recorded by
HELEN REDDY
on Capitol Records

WARNER BROS. MUSIC   CALEDONIA SOUL MUSIC & WB MUSIC CORP.

673715 - HELEN REDDY

The Music of Helen Reddy

A collection of Material

**Helen Reddy
Love Song
for
Jeffrey**

Songbook for Helen's first of two 1974 albums.
Her second album from 1974, "Free And Easy" also has a songbook.

Magazine Covers

→

Like sheet music and songbooks there are far too many magazines to be able to show them all. Of course I will not show the rag mag covers Helen has appeared on. This is merely a sample to showcase this amazing, beautiful and talented person!

January 23, 1978. 60¢

People

weekly

That uppity
butler on 'Soap'

A sex-symbol
heir to Sabich
hits the slopes

Benny Goodman,
swinging still

HELEN
REDDY

The Woman
roars softer
now—family
comes first,
and she's got
Jerry Brown's
ear

0   04

7724476

MAY 16, 1983 ■ $1.25

People weekly

Hollywood's Dirtiest Custody Case

Helen Reddy's fight for her son is embittered by violence, a break-in and a threatened young lover

0 10027

20

724414

50¢

SONG HITS

MAGAZINE JANUARY 1977

CDC 00043

CHARLTON
PUBLICATIONS

HELEN REDDY

BROTHERS JOHNSON

JOE STAMPLEY

WORDS TO OVER 60 HIT SONGS

POP

I GOT TO KNOW ● DON'T THINK ... FEEL ● FERNANDO ● QUEEN OF MY SOUL ● YOU ARE THE WOMAN ● TAKE A HAND ● LIKE A SAD SONG ● MUSKRAT LOVE

SOUL

THE RUBBERBAND MAN ● MR. MELODY ● MESSAGE IN OUR MUSIC ● CATFISH ● LET'S BE YOUNG TONIGHT ● JUST TO BE CLOSE TO YOU ● SUMMER

COUNTRY

I DON'T WANNA TALK IT OVER ANYMORE ● PEANUTS AND DIAMONDS ● ONE MORE TIME ● THAT LOOK IN HER EYES ● YOU AND ME ● AMONG MY SOUVENIRS ● HER NAME IS _____ ● THEY DON'T MAKE 'EM LIKE HER ANYMORE

DEDICATED TO THE NEEDS OF THE MUSIC/RECORD INDUSTRY

RECORD WORLD

WHO IN THE WORLD

'No Sad Song' is the Prophetic Title of Helen Reddy's New Capitol Single As Australian Thrush's Career—Guided By Husband Jeff Wald—Soars. New Reddy Album on Way, Too. Story Appears on Page 51.

NOVEMBER 20, 1971

PICKS OF THE WEEK

SINGLES

HELEN REDDY, "NO SAD SONG" (Screen Gems-Columbia, BMI). Songstress has been scoring every time out. This haunting melody perfect follow-up to "Crazy Love." Easy arrangement builds nicely into powerful refrain. Repeated listenings advised. Capitol 3231.

RARE EARTH, "HEY BIG BROTHER" (Jobete, BMI). Group has that can't miss formula, a natural follow-up to "I Just Want to Celebrate." They are one of the only "hard rock" groups consistently making it in top 40. B/w "Under God's Light" (Jobete, BMI). Rare Earth 5038F (Motown).

THE NITE-LITERS, "(We've Got To) PULL TO-GETHER" (Rutri, BMI). Group right back after "K-Jee." Wailing sax beginning eases into rock and roller in the old-time tradition. Excellent arrangement with many rhythm changes. B/w "Afro-Strut" (Rutri, BMI). RCA 74-0591.

BADFINGER, "DAY AFTER DAY" (Apple, ASCAP). This group has been releasing one single each year, and it never misses. This year should prove no exception. Produced in fine fashion by George Harrison. Flip produced by Todd Rundgren. B/w "Money" (Apple, ASCAP). Apple 1841.

SLEEPERS

DON McLEAN, "AMERICAN PIE" (Mayday, BMI). Artist is achieving tremendous airplay with this outing from LP cut. Monumental accomplishment of lyric writing. In a tribute to Buddy Holly McLean puts to rest many myths of the '60s. This record, although edited from original version, will make artist a major superstar. UA 50856.

TIN TIN, "SET SAIL FOR ENGLAND" (Casserole, BMI). Group that sounds like Bee Gees, Beatles and Moody Blues deserves notice. Just missing with "Is That the Way," they seem destined to be a major force in 1972. Their sound is consistent beauty with simple lyrics. In the long run, they must make it. Atco 45-6853.

COASTERS, "LOVE POTION NUMBER NINE" (Quintet, BMI). The Coasters are back with Leiber-Stoller smash of some years ago. New dimension added to original hit by Clovers, through the use of nifty percussion. Flip another Leiber-Stoller. B/w "D.W. Washburn" (Screen Gems-Columbia, BMI). King 45-6385. (Starday-King).

QUINCY JONES, "WHAT'S GOING ON (Parts I & II)" (Jobete, BMI). Marvin Gaye's smash comes back as a perfect jazz arrangement with MOR and pop flavor. Jones' sound is, as always original and distinct. Nice vocal back-up. From his latest "Smackwater Jack" LP. A&M 1316.

ALBUMS

GRAND FUNK RAILROAD, "E PLURIBUS FUNK." Grand Funk Railroad, who have made more money this year than just about any group, have fittingly packaged this new album like a coin. Certainly coins will flow in Grand Funk's direction for this one quickly. Grand Funk Railroad SW 853 (Capitol).

ELTON JOHN, "MADMAN ACROSS THE WATER." Elton John does some of his more important and introspective work on this package. He also does some of his best singing. Bernie Taupin also surpasses himself with his pungent, pellucid lyrics. Toos. Uni 93120 (MCA).

LED ZEPPELIN, UNTITLED ALBUM. Led Zeppelin haven't seen fit to title this package, preferring instead to provide a series of four identifying symbols. The first symbol looks like "Zoso," but obviously "Zoso" isn't a good title for such a fine album. Atlantic SD 7208.

JOHN DENVER, "AERIE." John Denver is hotter now than he's ever been and so the clamor for this album should be ear-splitting. The subtle, soft album is anything but ear-splitting. It's full of thoughtful, meaningful Denver-ish ballads. RCA LSP 4607.

Atlantic Promotes Greenberg, Vogel and Meyerson • **Barnaby Records Exits Nashville for West Coast** • **RCA Sponsors Free Concerts** • **Campus Report: Loyola Radio Conference** • **Dialogue: The Business of Blood, Sweat & Tears** • **RCA, Panasonic, JVC Report on 4-Channel**

SEPTEMBER 6, 1976

Woman's Day

40¢
(50c NZ)

THE TRUTH ABOUT
HELEN REDDY'S
MARRIAGE –
by the woman
who knows
her best

WHY
RESEARCHERS
SAY THERE
IS LIFE
AFTER
DEATH

DOCTOR
WRIGHT'S
HIGH
VITAMIN
HEALTH
PLAN

BUDGET
DECORATING:
25 brilliant
ideas PLUS
pullout
wallpaper book

CASH BOX

NEWSPAPER

July 31, 1976

$1.50

HELEN REDDY MAKES 'MUSIC, MUSIC'

CBS Convention Delegates Hear
Of Many Successes, Achievements

New CBS Label Plans Outlined

Retailers, Wholesalers Begin
Tracking Reggae Sales

Artists May Lose Out
Due To New Tax Treaty

WEA Income Highest Ever

Another Round in the
Creative/Financial Tussle (Ed)

SUNDAY NEWS

TV WEEK

JUNE 24 - 30, 1973

FLIP WILSON
Presents

Helen Reddy

Premieres Thursday

DEDICATED TO THE N[...] RECORD INDUSTRY

DECEMBER 28, 1974 $1.50

RECORD WORLD

YEAR END '74

Who In The World:

Helen Reddy

see page 20

HITS OF THE WEEK

SINGLES

CAROLE KING, "NIGHTINGALE" (prod. by Lou Adler) (Colgems, ASCAP). In top flight, the first lady of singer-song-writers combines melodic beauty with momentum extraordinaire to come up with a performance in super league with her recent chart-topper, "Jazzman." Here's more reason to smile from "Wrap Around Joy." Ode 66106 (A&M).

ANDY WILLIAMS, "LOVE SAID GOODBYE" (prod. by Marty & David Paich) (Famous, ASCAP). Hit man who added the first "Godfather" theme to his big-time film music repertoire comes up with the initial vocal version of the major ballad in the score of Paramount's cinema sequel. And so it's hello again to another movie monster. Columbia 3-10078.

HUDSON BROTHERS, "COOCHIE COOCHIE COO" (prod. by Hudson Bros. Prod.) (Lornhole, BMI). Sibling contingent had a long-running chart success with "So You Are a Star." Now they return with a twinkle in their eye and a tickle on their fingertips for the happily-rockin' follow-up from their "Hollywood Situation" sessions. Casablanca 816.

ABBA, "RING RING" (prod. by Bjorn Ulvaeus & Benny Anderson) (Overseas/Don Kirshner, BMI). The "Waterloo" gang follows the sweet pop of "Honey Honey" with a more hard-drivin' effort. Co-penned by Neil Sedaka, the song deals with a cold relationship and a silent telephone. Call it a top 40 chimer/charmer. Atlantic 3240.

SLEEPERS

DAVE MASON, "BRING IT ON HOME TO ME" (prod. by Dave Mason/Indaba Ent.) (Kags, BMI). Blues-tinged love song which the late Sam Cooke had a solid self-penned giant on in 1962 becomes a winner for Mason as easily as "Another Saturday Night" did for Cat Stevens; Dave brings it on home in renewed hit fashion. Columbia 3-10074.

HUGO MONTENEGRO, "THEME FROM THE GODFATHER PART II" (prod. by Dave Blume/Red River Prod.) (Famous, ASCAP). Instrumental theme from the film starring Al Pacino puts the orchestra leader in his greatest sales position since "The Good, the Bad and the Ugly." Electronically-generated sounds mesh effectively with sleek strings. RCA PB-10153.

JOE & BING, "ALASKA BLOODLINE" (prod. by Margo-Siegel-Margo) (KEC, ASCAP). The 49th State serves as a cool and crisp locale for a twosome produced by the guys who gave us Cross Country's "Midnight Hour." The time for a new folk-rock duo has long been at hand and it looks like J&B are just bound to fit the bill. Kirshner ZS8-4257 (Columbia).

BARRY RICHARDS, "BONNIE PLEASE DON'T GO (SHE'S LEAVING)" (prod. by Bobby Hart & Barry Richards: Father Productions/Gross Kupps Prod.) (Tree, BMI). The next potential giant from the man who wrote the current Mac Davis hit, Kevin Johnson. Countermelody of "Auld Lang Syne" gives this an additional edge for New Year's programming. A&M 1650.

ALBUMS

RUFUS Featuring CHAKA KHAN, "RUFUSIZED." Running away with two of Record World's Year End Awards, the sextet fulfills all promise previously exhibited, inevitably leading to a sure-fire smash set. Whether soulfully balladeering as on "Please Pardon Me," or rock 'n rolling as on "Half Moon" and "Right is Right," Rufus is a very special blend. ABC ABCD-837 (6.98).

MOTION PICTURE SOUNDTRACK, "LENNY." From Bob Fosse's fine film comes this soundtrack which mixes both music and stunning monologues extracted from Dustin Hoffman's superb performance, thus yielding a well-balanced dramatic/musical recording. A mighty Miles Davis selection, "It Never Entered My Mind," is included. UA UA-LA359-H (7.98).

CARL CARLTON, "EVERLASTING LOVE." In view of the sensation stirred by the album's title track (having become a top ten single), there's little doubt that the lp will do anything but fare likewise. Carlton's fervid vocal renditions enhance oldies and newies alike, most outstandingly "Signed, Sealed and Delivered," and "I Wanna Be Your Main Squeeze." ABC ABCD-857 (6.98).

KAYGEES, "KEEP ON BUMPIN' & MASTERPLAN." Fast disco favorites following in the footsteps of successful "older brother" group Kool & the Gang, this boogie band beats out r&b basics, embellished by their unique rhythm style, cohesively kept together by producer Ronald Bell. Both tunes listed have already made chart inroads. Gang 101 (PIP) (6.98).

Picture
Sleeves
&
Labels

→

Singles from around the globe!

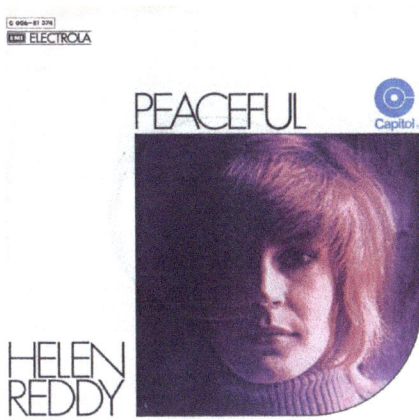

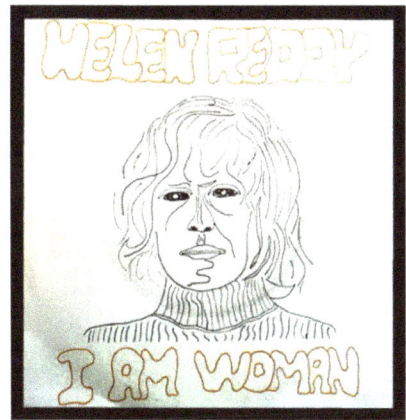

US, Germany, Japan, Netherlands... Helen's been loved everywhere!

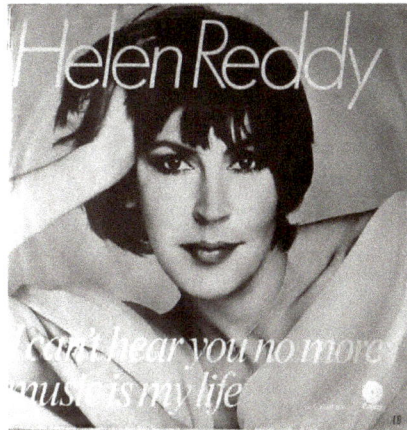

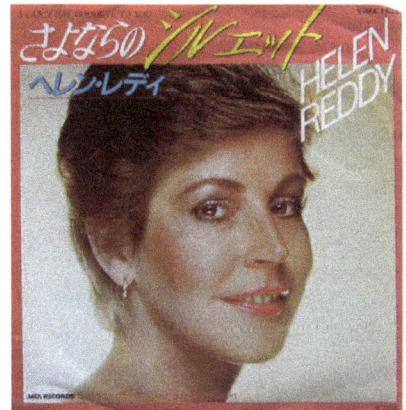

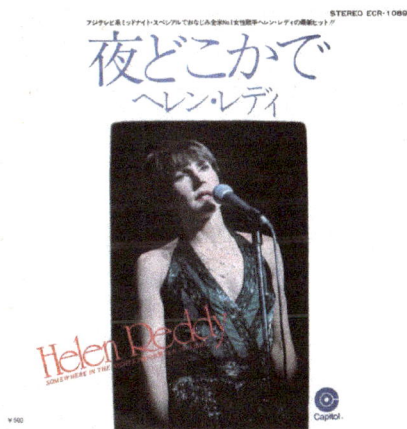

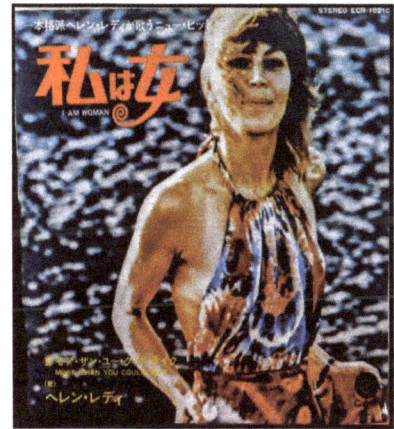

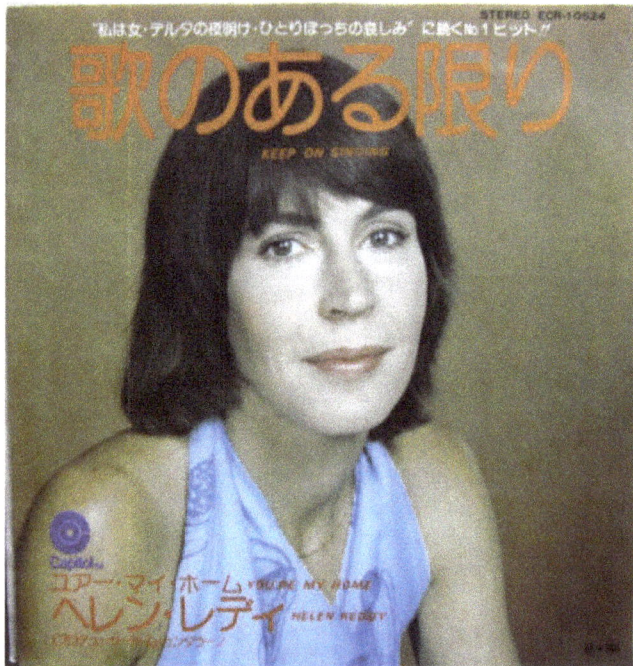

歌のある限り

KEEP ON SINGING

STEREO ECR-10524

"私は女・デルタの夜明け・ひとりぼっちの哀しみ" に続くNo.1ヒット"

ユアー・マイ・ホーム YOU'RE MY HOME
ヘレン・レディ HELEN REDDY

Helen
Reddy

KEEP ON
SINGING

Capitol
4 E006-81623

Helen Reddy

NO SAD SONG

MORE THAN YOU COULD TAKE

1 C006-81 019

Capitol

DELTA DAWN
(デルタの夜明け)
(A. Harvey-L. Collins)

A
STEREO
ECR-10411
(S45-90208)
45 r.p.m.
ASCAP

Produced by
Tom Catalano

United Artists
Music Co./
Big Ax Music
-ASCAP

HELEN REDDY
℗ 1973 Capitol Records, Inc.

Capitol®

CAPITOL MARCA REG. ALL RIGHTS RESERVED. UNAUTHORIZED DUPLICATION IS A VIOLATION OF APPLICABLE LAWS.

LAISSEZ LES
BONTEMPS ROULER
(C. Kelly-J. Didier)

★
NOT
FOR SALE

MONO

P-4487
PRO-8706

Intro.—:07
2:28

Bayou Blanc
Music, Inc./
Ertis Music
Co.-ASCAP

Produced by
Kim Fowley
& Earle
Mankey

(from the LP
"EAR
CANDY"
SO-11640)

HELEN REDDY
℗ 1977 Capitol Records, Inc.

MFD. BY CAPITOL RECORDS, INC., A SUBSIDIARY OF CAPITOL INDUSTRIES-EMI, INC.-U.S.A.

Capitol®

HEAVEN
RECORDS

Produced
by
Michael Lloyd
Michael Music
ASCAP

FOR
PROMOTIONAL
PURPOSES
ONLY

"YOU'RE THE ONE"
(Lloyd)
Helen Reddy & Tom Sullivan

14225 Ventura Blvd. Sherman Oaks, CA 91423
© 1982 Heaven Productions Inc.

CAPITOL
RECORDS
MONO

MASTER NO.   TIME
76384   2:48
PROJECT NO.   SIDE

45 RPM   33⅓ RPM

TITLE   CRAZY LOVE

ARTIST   HELEN REDDY

Form 5212 Rev. 6
10/68

CRAZY LOVE
(Van Morrison) (3:16)

Capitol

F.3138
(45.76384)

HELEN REDDY
Produced by LARRY MARKS

CRAZY LOVE
(Van Morrison)

STEREO   Warner Bros.
                Music/
                Van-Jan
                Music
                ASCAP 2:48

Capitol.   3138
                (45-76384)
                Produced by
                LARRY MARKS

(From the LP
"I DON'T
KNOW HOW TO
LOVE HIM"
ST-762)

HELEN REDDY

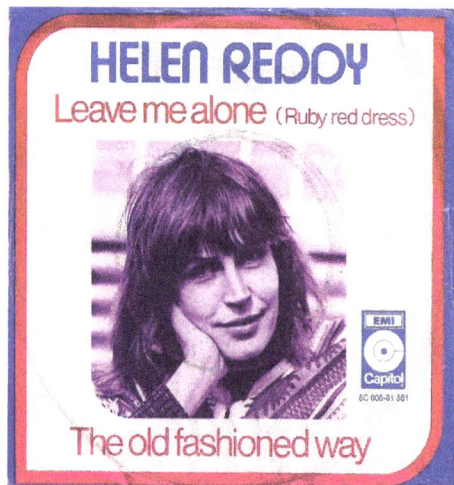

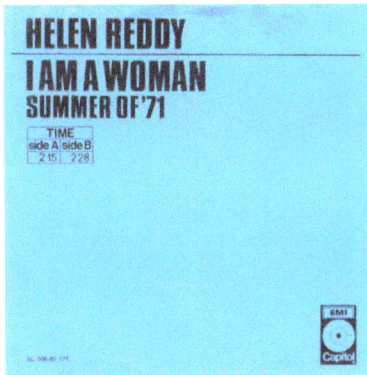

HELEN REDDY
I AM A WOMAN
SUMMER OF '71

TIME	
side A	side B
2 15	2 28

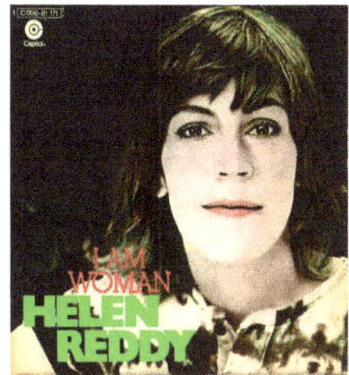

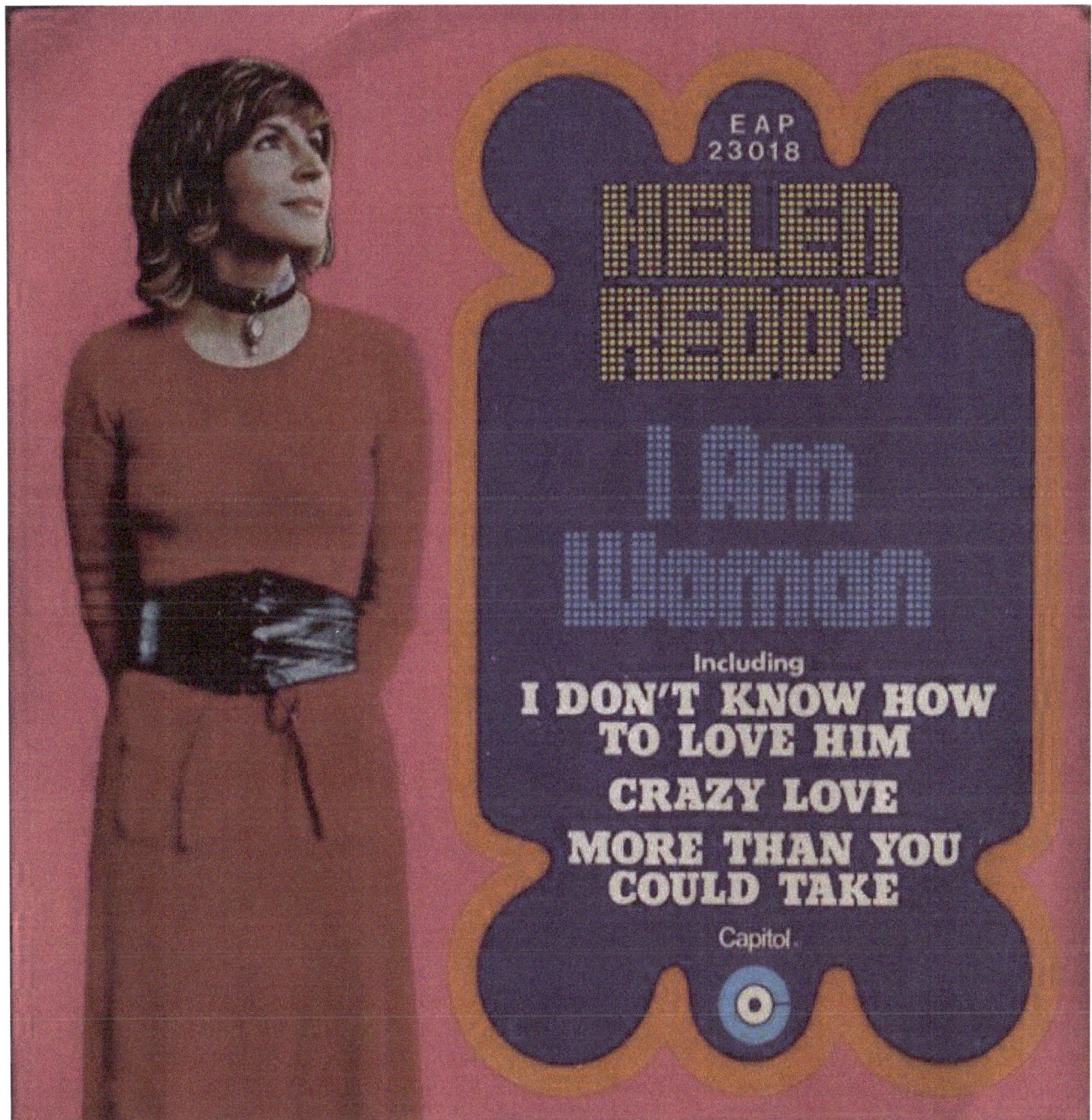

EAP
23018

HELEN
REDDY

I Am
Woman

Including

I DON'T KNOW HOW
TO LOVE HIM

CRAZY LOVE

MORE THAN YOU
COULD TAKE

Capitol

6E | 006-81374 |

HELEN REDDY
PEACEFUL

Capitol

WHAT WOULD
THEY SAY

HELEN REDDY

Peaceful
What whould they say

TIME	
side A	side B
250	245

EMI
Capitol

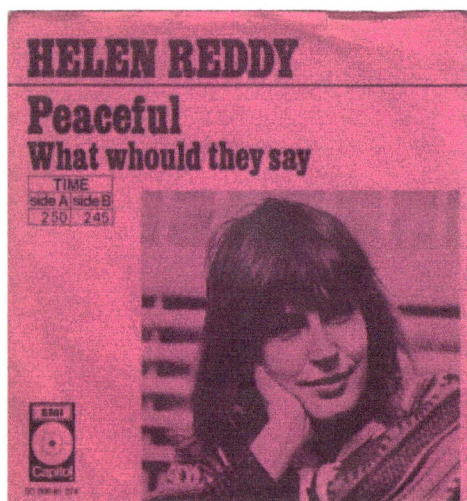

HELEN REDDY
Peaceful • What Would They Say

MOVIEPLAY / SN - 20.754

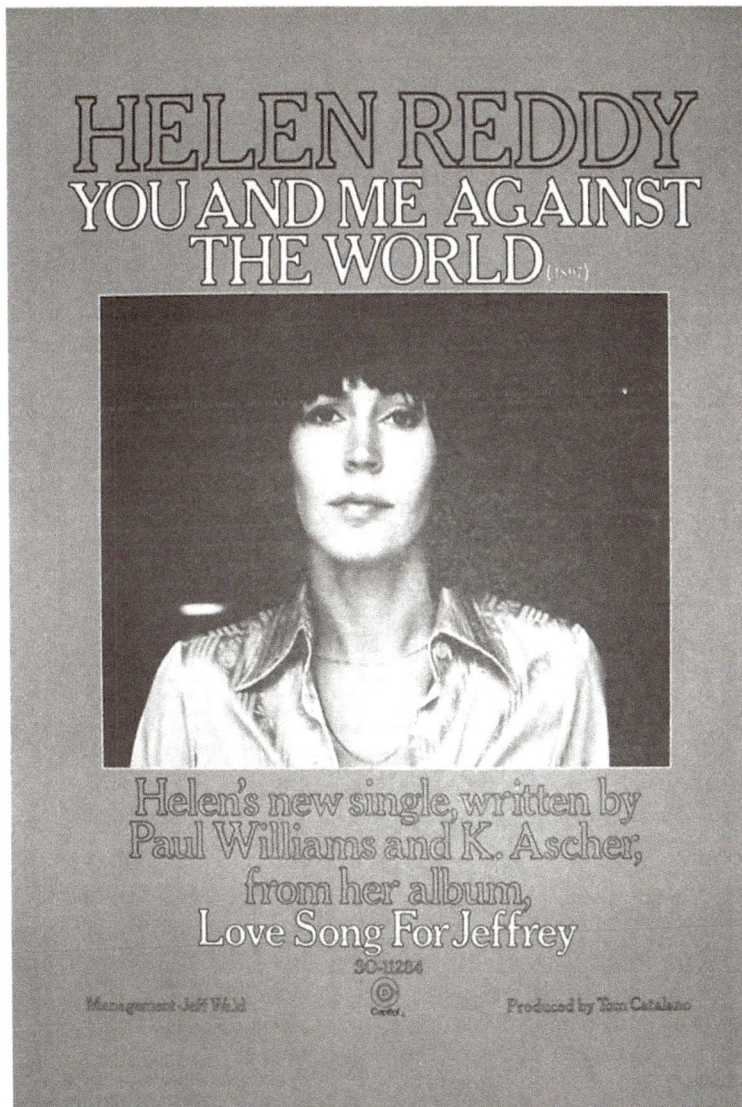

1 C 006-81 551
EMI ELECTROLA

HELEN REDDY

Leave Me Alone

Leave Me Alone (Ruby Red Dress)
(from the LP "Long Hard Climb")
(Linda Laurie)
HELEN REDDY
The Old Fashioned Way
(from the LP "Long Hard Climb")
(G. Garvarentz/A. Kasha/J. Hirschhorn)

Produced by Tom Catalano

STEREO 1 C 006-81 551 U
℗ 1973 "CAPITOL Records Inc."

Helen Reddy
Long Hard Climb

Neue LP von
HELEN REDDY:
„Long Hard Climb"
1C 062-81 493

EMI ELECTROLA
EMI Electrola GmbH, Köln. All rights reserved. Printed in Germany by Druckhaus Maack KG, 586 Lüdenscheid. Coverphoto: Capitol

HELEN REDDY
CANDLE ON THE WATER

From Walt Disney Productions'
PETE'S DRAGON

Capitol
RECORDS

© ℗ MCMLXXVII Walt Disney Productions

(4521)

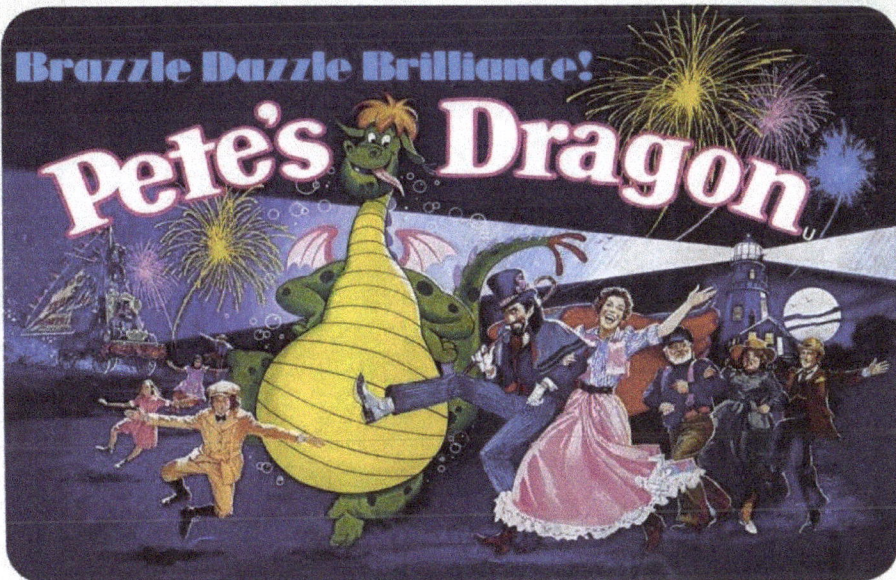

Brazzle Dazzle Brilliance!
Pete's Dragon

TECHNICOLOR ®   Your Campaign   ©1978 WALT DISNEY PRODUCTIONS (see page 23)

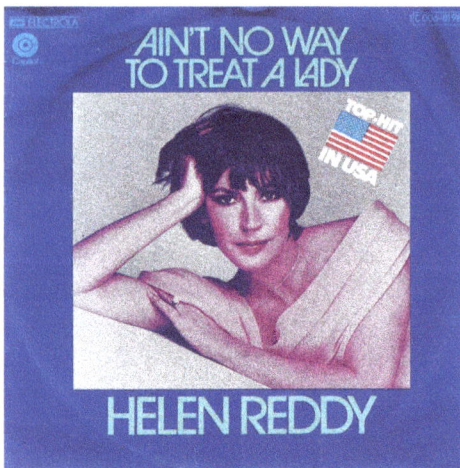

EMI ELECTROLA

MAKE LOVE TO ME

Helen Reddy

1C 052-85955 YZ

12" MAXI SINGLE

Capitol

Capitol
REG. U.S. PAT. OFF.

MFD. BY CAPITOL RECORDS, INC., A SUBSIDIARY OF CAPITOL INDUSTRIES-EMI, INC., U.S.A.

©1979 Capitol
Records, Inc.

STEREO

4712
S95776A

(from the
forthcoming
LP "REDDY"

Trajor
Music Co.
ASCAP

TIME
3:48

Produced by
Frank Clay
Associate
Producer
Bruce Sperling

HELEN REDDY
MAKE LOVE TO ME
(Yellowstone-Voice-Tinsley)

Capitol MARCA REG. • ALL RIGHTS RESERVED. UNAUTHORIZED DUPLICATION IS A VIOLATION OF APPLICABLE LAWS.

Helen's 1979 single of "Wonder Child" b/w "I Make Up Songs" (CTW 199073)
Taken from the Sesame Street album
"The Stars Come Out On Sesame Street"
(LP CTW 79007)

(Cassette C-79007)

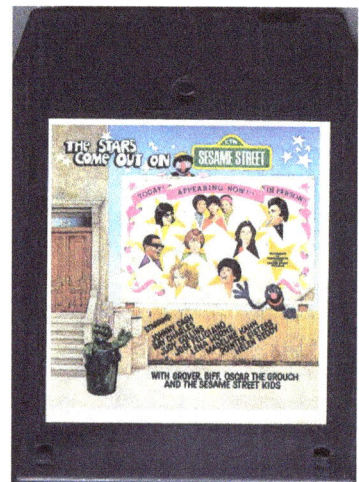

(8-Track 8T-79007)

STEREO ECR-10411

(助)ヘレン
レディ

ゴスペルのフィーリング
ヘレン・レディの
新しい魅力が花開く！

デルタ
の夜明け

友達ならば

DELTA DAWN

IF WE COULD STILL BE
FRIENDS

¥500

Capitol

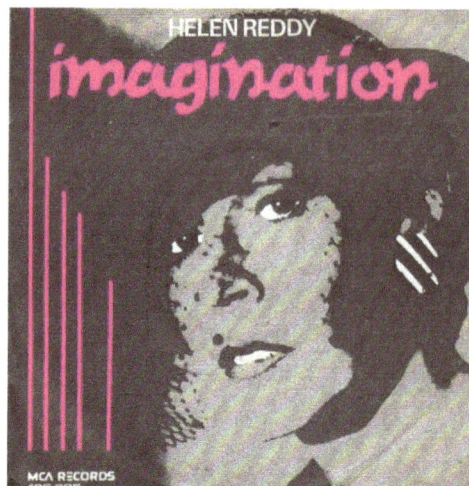

HELEN REDDY
imagination

MCA RECORDS
105-325

£2·50

I Can't Say Goodbye To You

HELEN
REDDY

Save Me

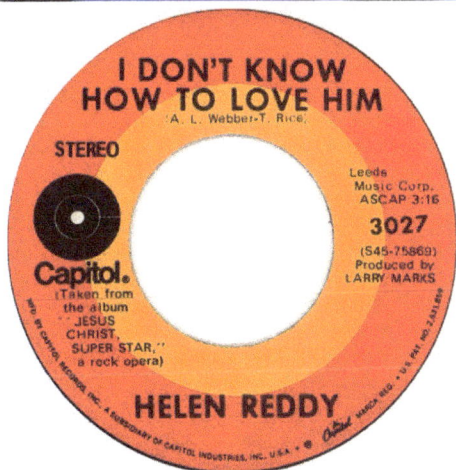

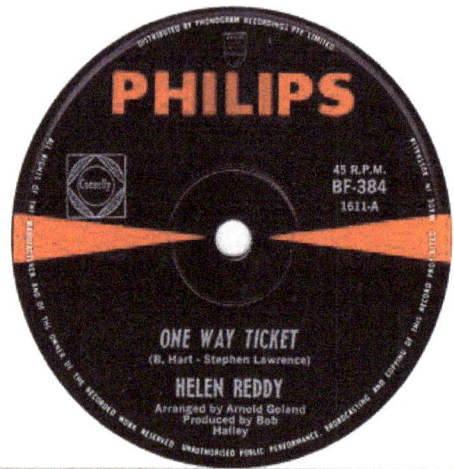

Poland picture card with Helen's "Angie Baby"
Cute cat...

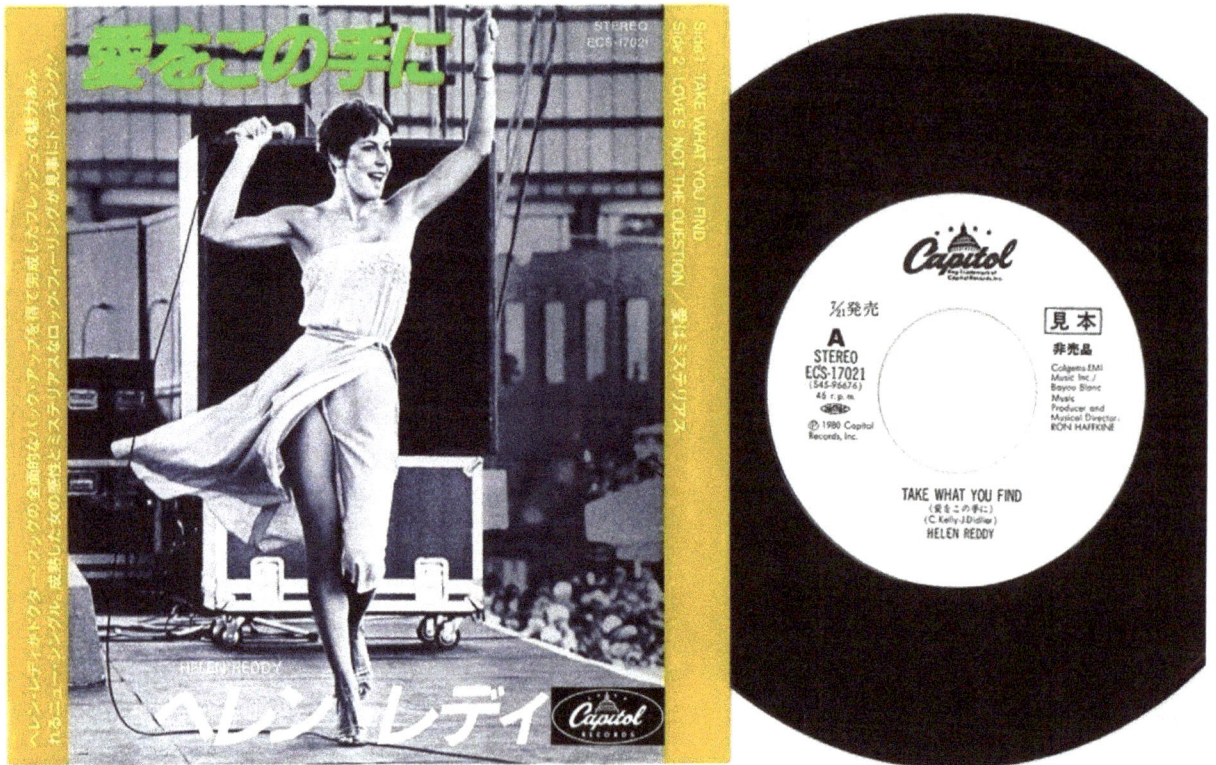

"Take What You Find" Japanese promotional single 1980

"We'll Sing In The Sunshine" Japanese promotional single 1978

ELECTROLA
Capitol
1C 006·82 300

Helen Reddy
I Can't Hear You No More

STEREO ECR-10411

(歌)ヘレン
レディ

ゴスペルのフィーリング
ヘレン・レディの
新しい魅力が花開く！

デルタ
の夜明け
友達ならば

DELTA DAWN
IF WE COULD STILL BE
FRIENDS

Capitol
¥500

ELECTROLA
1C 006·EA 162

HELEN REDDY

Take What You Find

Love's Not The Question

Capitol

RELEASED BY
Rothmans of Pall Mall
(AUST.) LTD.

CONSULATE

SPEED: 45 R.P.M.

GETAWAY

N21718

BOB YOUNG AND HIS ORCHESTRA
VOCAL: HELEN REDDY

(Arr. Bob Young)

UNAUTHORISED COPYING, PUBLIC PERFORMANCE AND BROADCASTING OF THIS RECORD PROHIBITED

EMI ELECTROLA
Capitol

Helen Reddy

keep on singing

Promotional Materials

→

Some can also be seen in the Photo Gallery section!

HELEN REDDY

in

BLOOD Brothers

The Hit Musical by
WILLY RUSSELL

"UNBEATABLE!"
–Sheridan Morley, International Herald Tribune

MUSIC BOX THEATRE
239 West 45th Street
Tele-charge®: (212) 239-6200

2ND SENSATIONAL YEAR!

The staff and friends at
Irving Music
wish to congratulate
Helen Reddy
on her number 1 single
"I Am Woman"

Irving Music (BMI)/Almo Music (ASCAP)/The Rondor Group
PUBLISHERS OF FINE MUSIC

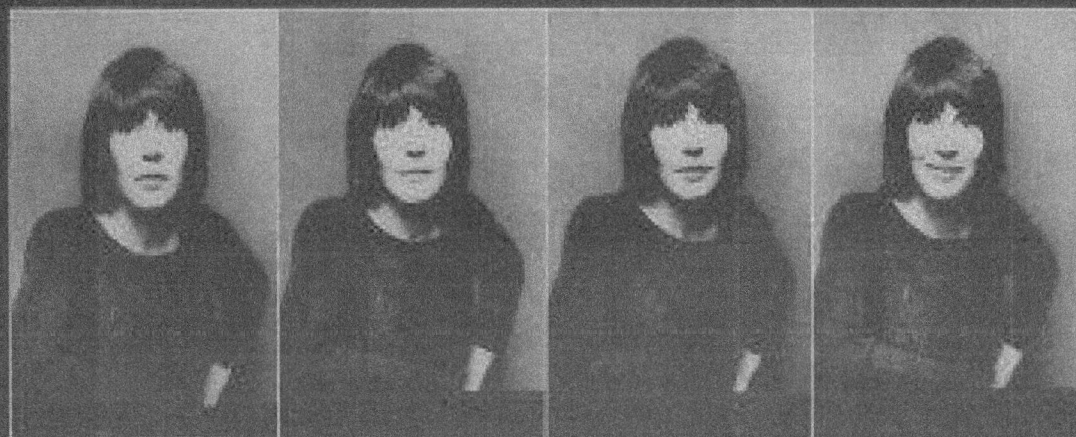

Mother's Day Eve

HELEN REDDY

at the
KAHALA
Mandarin Oriental

MAY 8
Saturday • 8pm

Tickets on Sale Now
Hotel Lobby &
Blaisdell Box Office
Charge-by-phone 526-4400

Week of July 1st, 1973: "The Helen Reddy Show:" Yes, this is the
young lady who wrote "I Am a Woman," currently the national anthem
of the fem-lib movement, however, those who expect her to come on
like Bella Abzug are in for disappointment. Ms Reddy makes a much
softer presentation than one would suspect and as she states "I Am
a Woman" it seems like a rather nice thing to be. NBC-TV evidently
thought so too for they are presenting her 8-week music & comedy
series as the summer replacement for Flip Wilson. It can be seen
Thursdays, 8-9 p.m. ET during the run.

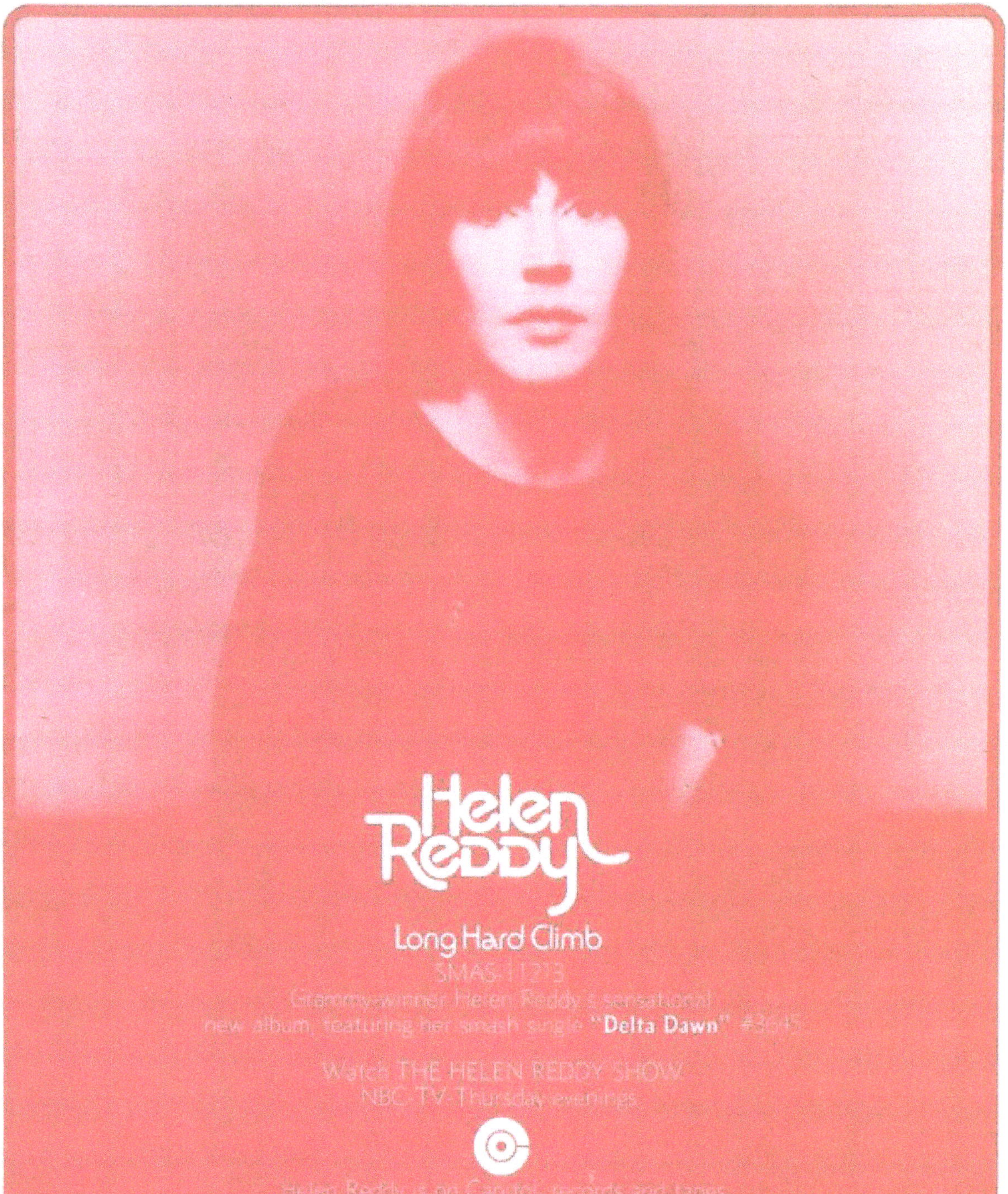

Helen in 1973

TV
• Free every Sunday with your Chicago Sun-Times

prevue

HELEN REDDY

MCA Welcomes Helen Reddy

Helen Reddy was recently welcomed to MCA Records' national headquarters in
Angeles, where she discussed her upcoming debut album on the label, scheduled
late spring. Pictured, from left, are: Pat Pipolo, vice president of promotion; Bob Sin
president of MCA Records; Reddy; her manager, Jeff Wald; Lou Cook, vice president
worldwide business affairs; Denny Rosencrantz, vice president of A&R; and Redd
producer, Joel Diamond.

Sorry about the text cut off at either side above. This is here for the historical significance.

Pete's Dragon promotion kit

WALT DISNEY PRODUCTIONS' PETE'S DRAGON   TECHNICOLOR® G

DEREK BLOCK Presents

HELEN REDDY
IN CONCERT 1980

Helen on The Love Boat

Midnight Special

Unfortunately the song "You're The One" sung by Helen and Tom Sullivan has never been officially released on vinyl or CD.

AN ALL-STAR CAST IN A FOUR-STAR MOVIE!

AIRPORT 1975

CHARLTON HESTON
KAREN BLACK · GEORGE KENNEDY · GLORIA SWANSON
EFREM ZIMBALIST, JR. · SUSAN CLARK · SID CAESAR · LINDA BLAIR
DANA ANDREWS · ROY THINNES · NANCY OLSON · ED NELSON
MYRNA LOY · AUGUSTA SUMMERLAND and HELEN REDDY

Written by DON INGALLS · Inspired by the novel "AIRPORT" by Arthur Hailey
Directed by JACK SMIGHT · Music by JOHN CACAVAS · Produced by WILLIAM FRYE
A UNIVERSAL PICTURE · TECHNICOLOR "PANAVISION"

ORIGINAL SOUNDTRACK AVAILABLE EXCLUSIVELY ON MCA RECORDS AND TAPES

PRINTED IN U.S.A.

Helen front and center with other Grammy winners in a promotional-only photo in 1983. Helen hosted the program a few times. Karen Carpenter is seen four rows up in what would turn out to be one of her final public appearances. Sadly she would collapse and die a few weeks later.

JAZZ
CLASSICS

SIDE A

JAZZCLASS
45 001

HELEN REDDY
Hit The Road Jack

Promotional Radio Use Only Not For Resale

This 45 RPM single, available in various colors, is rumored to be a UK bootleg. It was reportedly pressed in 2009, 2011, 2013 and 2015. The flip side is Salena Jones "Right Now."

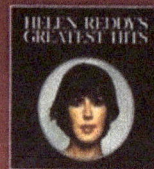

A 1977 album promotional poster from
Capitol Records.

Compilation Albums

→

This is not all the compilation albums released on Helen Reddy, only a sampling. Like any other popular artist there are many, many released in various parts of the world by many different companies who licensed the original recordings. These releases are usually titled "Best Of," "Greatest Hits," "Gold," "Top Hits," etc. Not all these compilations are released to the public. Some are meant for promotional use only.

Greatest Hits
ST 23610

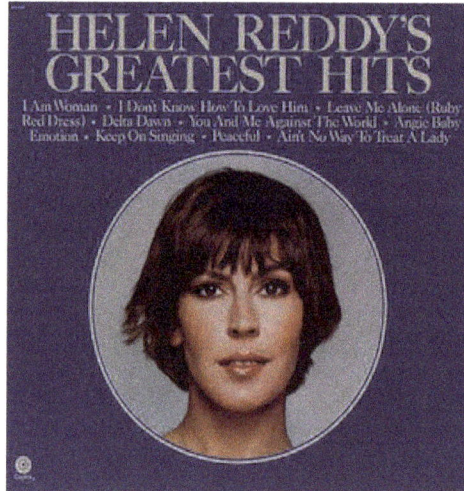

Track Listing:
I Am Woman / I Don't Know How To Love Him / Leave Me Alone (Ruby Red Dress) / Delta Dawn / You And Me Against The World / Angie Baby / Emotion / Keep On Singing / Peaceful / Ain't No Way To Treat A Lady

Production Information:
Produced by: Tom Catalano, except: Larry Marks ("I Don't Know How to Love Him") / Jay Senter ("I Am Woman") / Joe Wissert ("Angie Baby," "Emotion," "Ain't No Way to Treat a Lady")
Recorded at: A&M Studios, Capitol Recording Studios and Sunwest Studios, Hollywood, CA
Cover Photography: Francesco Scavullo
Art Direction: Roy Kohara

Album Data:
Billboard Chart Debut (US): December 6, 1975
Highest Chart Position: 5 (US) 9 (Canada)
Billboard Chart: Top 200 Albums
Number of weeks on Chart: 51

Notes / Trivia:

- This album was released on LP, 8-Track, Open Reel and Cassette Tape on November 15, 1975.
- It achieved Gold status on December 3, 1975 and Double Platinum status on February 5, 1992.
- In the UK this album was titled "The Best of Helen Reddy." It peaked at # 5 on the UK's "Official Charts Company." It used the same cover artwork.
- In New Zealand the album topped the charts at # 1.
- In 1987 an edition was released on LP and CD in several countries with extra tracks and titled *Helen Reddy's Greatest Hits (And More).* It was the first release of the original compilation on compact disc. On April 14, 1997, that edition was reissued once more and re-titled *Love Songs*. The extra tracks were: "Somewhere in the Night" / "I Can't Hear You No More" / "You're My World" / "The Happy Girls" / "Make Love to Me."

Lust For Life
PDL2-1066

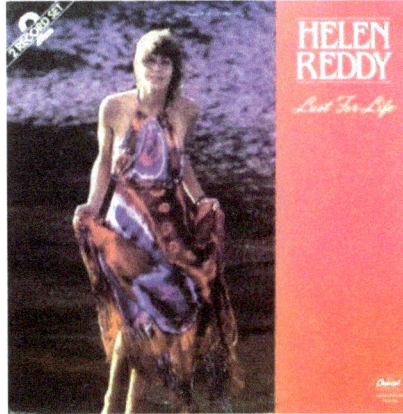

Track Listing:

I Am Woman / Delta Dawn / You're My World / We'll Sing In The Sunshine / Angie Baby / Candle On The Water / Somewhere In The Night / Emotion / Ain't No Way To Treat A Lady / Leave Me Alone (Ruby Red Dress) / Love's Not The Question / All I Ever Need / I've Been Wanting You So Long / Think I'll Write A Sing / And I Love You So / I Don't Know How To Love Him

Production Information:

Cover Photography: Don Peterson

Notes / Trivia:

- This album was released on double LP in September 1984
- This 2 LP (1 CD) set contains material from 1971- 1980.
- The label claims this is the equivalent of 2 albums but there are only 16 songs, not 20.
- Manufactured by: Capitol Records, Inc.
- Manufactured by: CEMA Special Markets
- LP's Pressed by: Capitol Records Pressing Plant, Jacksonville, Illinois (Opened on July 12, 1965, closed in 2004)
- Cover photograph was taken at the same session as Helen's second LP "Helen Reddy" in 1971.

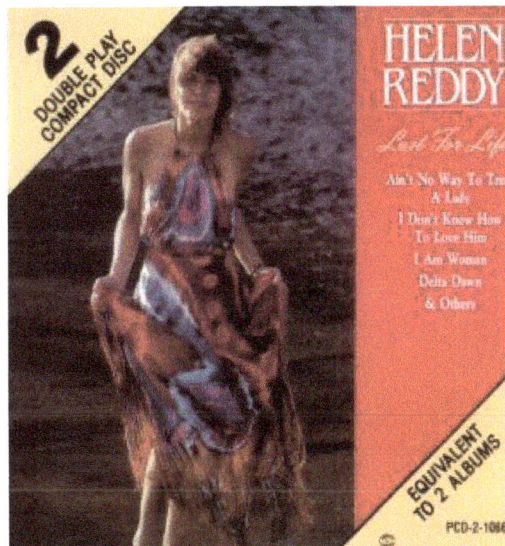

The compact disc cover showing slightly different graphics.

The Best of Helen Reddy
PLAY-260079

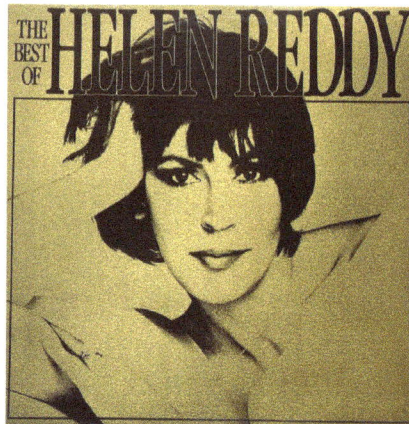

Track Listing:
I Am Woman / This Masquerade / Keep On Singing / I Don't Know How To Love Him / Minute By minute / I Believe In Music / Peaceful / I'll Be Your Audience / Ain't No Way To Treat A Lady / Free And Easy / Delta Dawn / Emotion / Words Are Not Enough / Leave Me Alone (Ruby Red Dress) / You And Me Against The World / Angie Baby / You're So Good / Imagination / Love Song For Jeffrey

Production Information:
Mastered by: Allan Parsons at Studios 301 in Sydney, Australia.
Cover photograph: Francesco Scavullo. 1975.

Notes / Trivia:
- This album was released on LP and Cassette in July 1984 and CD in 1991.
- Manufactured By: EMI Manufacturing Pty. Ltd. Australia.
- Marketed By: EMI Retail Promotions
- The cover photograph may look familiar as it is the same as the one used on Helen's 1975 album "Ain't No Way To Treat A Lady."
- A similar version of the album was released in Australia in 1991, also by EMI, with the same cover art, but with tracks switched around or replaced.

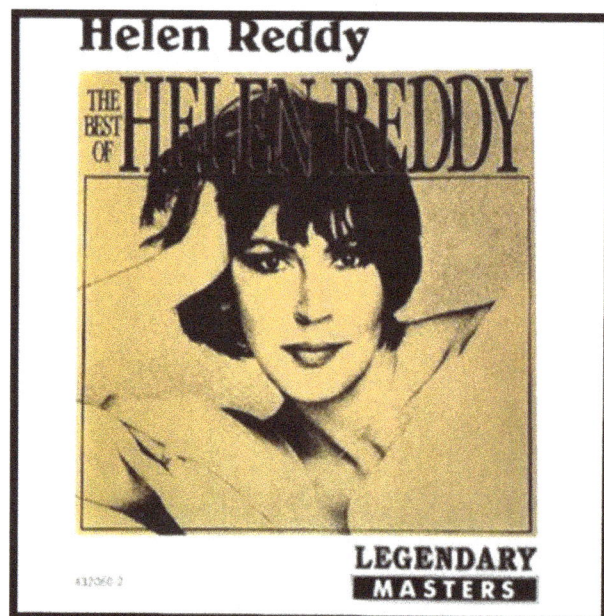

The 1991 CD cover artwork

Helen Reddy's Greatest Hits (And More)
EKPL-0065

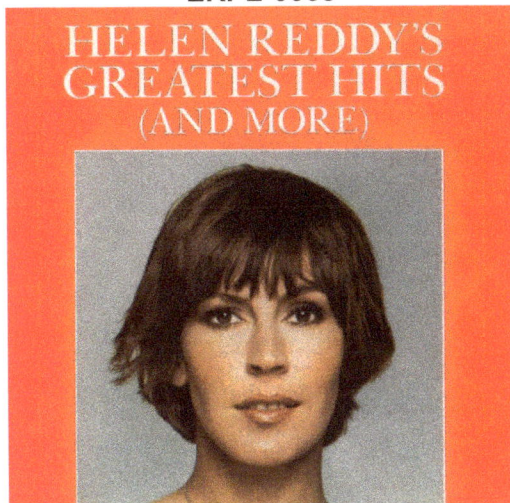

Track Listing:

I Am Woman / I Don't Know How To Love Him / Leave Me Alone (Ruby Red Dress) / Delta Dawn / The Happy Girls / Angie Baby / Make Love To Me / Keep On Singing / Peaceful / Ain't No Way To Treat A Lady / Somewhere In The Night / I Can't Hear You No More / You're My World / You And Me Against The World / Emotion

Production Information:

Photography: Cover: Francesco Scavullo / Back insert: Claude Mougin

Notes / Trivia:

- This album was released in November 1987 on LP and on CD on October 25, 1990.
- This is the EMI/Kemongsa version from Asia. It includes an 11" x 11" insert with bio and a near full page B&W photograph on the opposite side of the cover photo. This is an authorized release.
- There are other versions using this same cover art with tracks replaced or moved around from Japan, USA as well as other countries.

Back of CD insert with tracks re-arranged

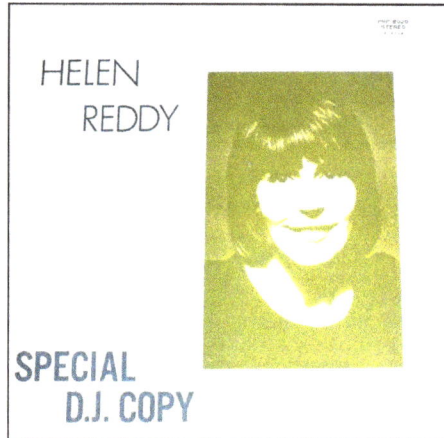

Track Listing:

HELEN REDDY:
Keep On Singing / I Am Woman / I Don't Know How To Love Him / Crazy Love / This Masquerade / The Old Fashioned Way / Peaceful / Delta Dawn / Leave Me Alone (Ruby Red Dress) / Until It's Time For You To Go / And I Love You So / No Sad Songs / Long Hard Climb / You're My Home

ANNE MURRAY:
Love Song / Just One Look / Danny's Song / Snowbird / Killing Me Softly With His Song / Cotton Jenny / Destiny / I'll Never Fall In Love Again

GLEN CAMPBELL:
By The Time I Get To Phoenix / Houston / Gentle On My Mind / Wichita Line Man / Galveston / It's Only Make Believe / dream Baby (How Long Must I Dream) / Your Cheatin' Heart

Notes / Trivia:
- This double LP was pressed in Japan and only released to radio and reviewers there in May 1974. Helen has a whole two sides on the first LP and Anne and Glen share the second LP with sides of their own. Helen graces the cover alone and Anne and Glen share the back jacket. Inside the gate fold there is information on each track and a bio for each Capitol artist. Albums and singles for each artist are also highlighted. This set in recent years was very hard to come by unless you spent a a small fortune.

The back jacket showing Anne Murray and Glen Campbell

MOR – Special D.J. Copy
PRP-8035

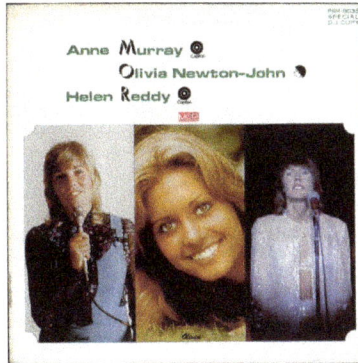

Track Listing:

HELEN REDDY:
Angie Baby / I Am Woman / Delta Dawn / Leave Me Alone (Ruby Red Dress) / Keep On Singing / I Don't Know How To Love Him

ANNE MURRAY:
Day Tripper / Dream Lover / Snowbird / Love Song / Danny's Song

OLIVIA NEWTON-JOHN:
Let Me Be There / I Honestly Love You / If You Love Me (Let Me Know) / If Not For You / Long Live Love

Notes / Trivia:
- This special DJ album was made in Japan for radio and reviewers. Going by the song selections this was pressed in 1974. While Helen and Anne were both on Capitol, Olivia was on EMI (MCA).
- "Sample Disc" is printed on both sides of the LP in Japanese. "Not for Sale" is printed on back sleeve also in Japanese.
- This album also sells for a fair amount due to the fact that not many were pressed.

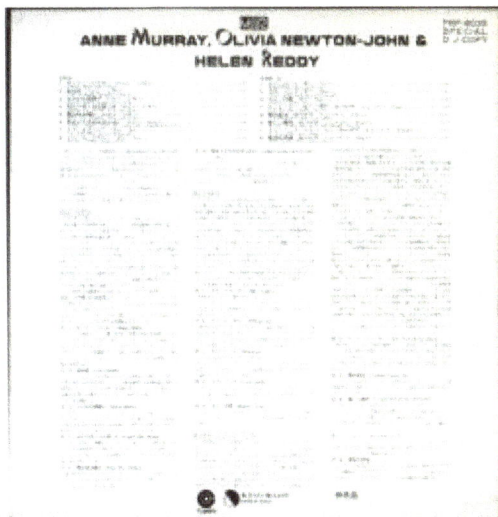

The back jacket and Side One label.

Helen Reddy / Shirley Bassey / Dusty Springfield
SPC-3356

Track Listing:

HELEN REDDY:
One Way Ticket / Go / The Junk Man's Serenade

SHIRLEY BASSEY:
The Wayward Wind / How About You / As I Love You

DUSTY SPRINGFIELD:
I Only Want To Be With You / Live It Up / You Don't Own Me

Notes / Trivia:
- This is a September 1973 compilation album which highlighted early original Philips and Fontana recordings by Helen Reddy, Shirley Bassey and Dusty Springfield. The Helen Reddy tracks are her first recordings all from 1968 - two of which were issued on the Fontana label.
- The album was available on LP, 8-Track and Cassette Tape.
- Some tracks electronically enhanced to simulate stereo.

Side One of the release featuring Helen's tracks

The Best of Helen Reddy
5C054-81 467

Track Listing:

I Don't Know How To Love Him / Crazy Love / How Can I Be Sure / Our House / I Am Woman / I Don't Remember My Childhood / No Sad Song / A Song For You / Don't Make Promises / I Believe In Music / Best Friend / Peaceful

Notes / Trivia:

- This compilation was issued in June 1973 to tie in with Helen's growing popularity in Europe.
- Vervaardigd in licentie door N.V. Bovema Holland = Manufactured under license by N.V. Bovema Holland

THE BEST OF HELEN REDDY

5C054-81 467

Side 1	Time
1. I don't know how to love him (From the Rock Opera „Jesus Christ", Superstar)	-3:15-A. L. Webber-T. Rice
2. Crazy love	-3:16-Van Morrison
3. How can I be sure	-2:50-F. Cavaliere-E. Brigati
4. Our house	-2:58-Graham Nash
5. I am woman	-3:24-H. Reddy-R. Burton
6. I don't remember my childhood	-3:30-Leon Russell

Side 2	Time
1. No sad song	-3:09-C. King-T. Stern
2. A song for you	-3:03-Leon Russell
3. Don't make promises	-3:02-Tim Hardin
4. I believe in music	-3:14-Mac Davis
5. Best friend	-2:17-H. Reddy-R. Burton
6. Peaceful	-2:50-Kenny Rankin

All selections produced by Larry Marks except I am woman by Jay Senter and Peaceful by Tom Catalano.

MORE HELEN REDDY ALBUMS ON CAPITOL

HELEN REDDY
Time - How? - Come on John - Summer of '71 - I don't remember my childhood - No sad song - I think it's going to rain today - Tulsa turnaround - More than you could take - New Year's resovolution
Capitol 5C052.81 024

HELEN REDDY I AM WOMAN
Peaceful - I am woman - This masquerade - I didn't mean to love you - Where is my friend - And I love you so - What would they say - Where is the love - Hit the road, Jack - The last blues song
Capitol 5C062.81 311

Manufactured by B.V. Bovema-Holland

The back jacket which strangely does not feature Helen's first album though this album contains material from it!

Helen Reddy's Greatest Hits
ST 23610

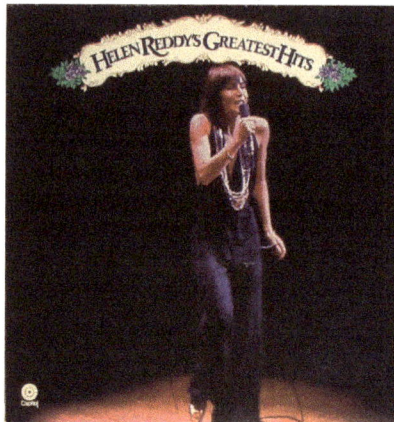

Track Listing:

I Don't Know How To Love Him / No Sad Song / Peaceful / Summer Of '71 / I Am Woman / Leave Me Alone (Ruby Red Dress) / Delta Dawn / Keep On Singing / You And Me Against The World / Angie Baby / Free And Easy / Bluebird

Notes / Trivia:

- This compilation was issued October 4, 1975 in New Zealand in limited numbers.
- Tracks A1, A2, A4, A5; ℗ 1971 / Track A3 - ℗ 1972 / Tracks A6, B1 - ℗ 1973 / Tracks B2 - B5 - ℗ 1974, Track B6 - ℗ 1975

  "Dedicated to Jeff, Tracy and Jordan"

  "Peaceful," "I Am Woman" from the album "I Am Woman." ST-11068

  "Angie Baby," "Free And Easy," from the album "Free And Easy." ST-11348

  "Leave Me Alone (Ruby Red Dress)," "Delta Dawn," from the album "Long Hard Climb." SMAS-11213

  "Bluebird," from the album "No Way To Treat A Lady." ST-11418

  "Keep On Singing," "You And Me Against The World," from the album "Love Song For Jeffrey." SO-11284

  "Summer Of '71," "No Sad Song," from the album "Helen Reddy." ST-857

  "I Don't Know How To Love Him," from the album "I Don't Know How To Love Him." ST-762
- Marketed by EMI New Zealand Limited, P.O. Box 30-476, Lower Hutt.
- Producers: Joe Wissert (tracks: B4, B5, B6), Larry Marks (tracks: A1, A2, A4, A6) and Tom Catalano (tracks: A3, A5, B1, B2, B3)

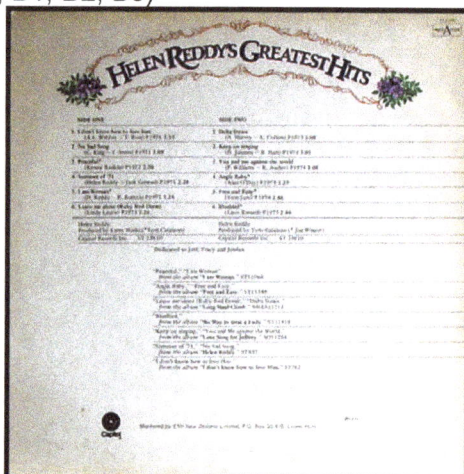

The back jacket for the New Zealand Greatest Hits compilation.

The Woman I Am: The Definitive Collection
09463-57613-2-0

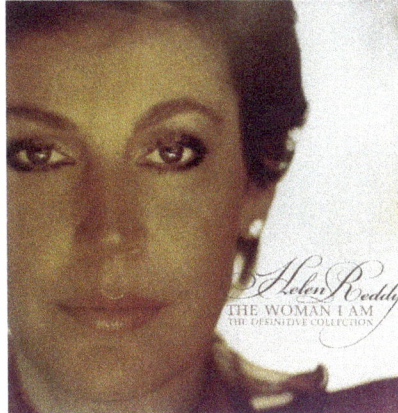

Track Listing:

I Don't Know How to Love Him / Crazy Love / Best Friend / I Am Woman / Peaceful / Delta Dawn / Leave Me Alone (Ruby Red Dress) / Keep On Singing / You and Me Against the World / I Think I'll Write a Song / Angie Baby / Emotion / Bluebird / Ain't No Way to Treat a Lady / Somewhere in the Night / I Can't Hear You No More / You're My World / Candle on the Water (from *Pete's Dragon*) / We'll Sing in the Sunshine / The West Wind Circus (live 1978) / Mama (live 1978) / Surrender

Production Information:

Original Producer: Tom Catalano, except: Kim Fowley ("You're My World," "We'll Sing in the Sunshine") / Kasha, Michael Lloyd & Mike Curb ("Candle on the Water") / Earle Mankey ("You're My World") / Larry Marks ("Best Friend," "Crazy Love," "I Don't Know How to Love Him") / John Palladino, Helen Reddy ("Mama," "The West Wind Circus") / Jay Senter ("I Am Woman") / Joe Wissert ("Angie Baby," "Emotion," "I Think I'll Write a Song," "Bluebird," "Ain't No Way to Treat a Lady," "Somewhere in the Night," "I Can't Hear You No More")
Compilation Producer: Kevin Flaherty
Cover Photo: Douglas Kirkland / Additional Photography: Peter Borsari / Gunther
Mastered by: David McEowen at Capitol Mastering Studios, Hollywood, California
Track / Liner Notes: Helen Reddy
Art Direction: Susan Lavoie
Design: Steve Silvas
Music Consultant: Jordan Sommers

Notes / Trivia:

- This compilation album was issued by Capitol Records on May 2, 2006 to tie in with Helen's autobiography "The Woman I Am" published by Jeremy P. Tarcher / Penguin in 2006 (US)
- AllMusic review by Rob Theakston read: "Most people typically regard Helen Reddy's "I Am Woman" as the quintessential anthem for the women's liberation movement in America during the '70s. But sadly for mainstream audiences, Reddy is a '70s one-hit wonder; nothing could be further from the truth. This 22-track session, Woman I Am: Definitive Collection, serves to set the record straight with a comprehensive overview of her adult contemporary chart hits from her tenure at Capitol Records during the '70s. All of her most well-known hits are here including (of course) "I Am Woman," "I Don't Know How to Love Him," "Angie Baby," and "Delta Dawn," all of which cracked the Billboard Top Ten singles chart, but there are also minor hits and fan favorites which complement the collection of hits quite well. Complete with liner notes from Reddy herself, this is quite possibly the most comprehensive collection of her material that a casual fan could possibly ever need, and something which die-hard fans will enjoy having around, if only to have all of her most important works together in one volume."

Rarities from the Capitol Vaults
CCM-2014

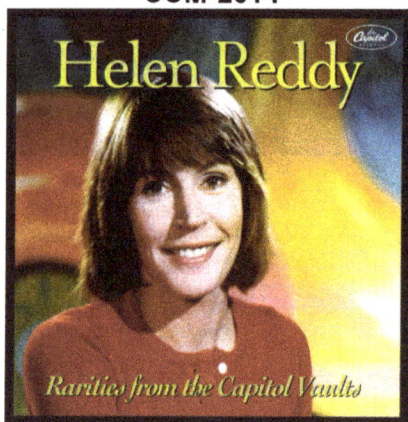

Track Listing:

I Am Woman (alternate version) from sessions for the 1971 album *I Don't Know How to Love Him* / Me And My Love from sessions for the 1978 album *We'll Sing In The Sunshine* / Together from sessions for the 1978 album *We'll Sing In The Sunshine* / Rhythm Rhapsody from sessions for the 1978 album *We'll Sing In The Sunshine* / Blue (alternate version) from sessions for the 1978 album *We'll Sing In The Sunshine* / Tell Jack no information available / Exhaustion from sessions for the 1979 album *Reddy* / Don't Mess With A Woman (alternate version) from the April 23, 1972 session in which "I Am Woman" was re-recorded for the single release / Lullaby no information available / Songs (alternate version) from sessions for the 1974 album *Love Song For Jeffrey* / Take What You Find (extended mix) promotional-only, extended 12" disco edition / Plus de Chansons Tristes (No Sad Song) The English-language version appears on the 1971 album *Helen Reddy.* This track was released as a single in Europe only in 1971.

Production Information:

Original Producers: Tom Catalano ("Songs") / Frank Day ("Exhaustion") / Kim Fowley ("Me and My Love," "Together," "Rhythm Rhapsody," "Blue") / Ron Haffkine ("Take What You Find") / Larry Marks ("I Am Woman," "Plus de Chansons Tristes") / Jay Senter ("Don't Mess with a Woman")
Compilation Producer: Jim Pierson
Associate Producer: Matt Tunia
Executive Producer: Gordon Anderson
Cover photograph Courtesy Of: CEA/Cache Agency
Liner Notes: Mike Ragogna, April 2009
Master tape assemblage and preparation: Dennis Jay
Mastered at Capitol Mastering Studios, Hollywood, California
Mastered by: David McEowen

Notes / Trivia:

- This compilation album was released on CD on July 21, 2009.

Best 20
ECS-90020

Track Listing:

Keep On Singing / I Am Woman / I Don't Know How To Love Him / No Sad Song / Peaceful / I Got A Name / This Masquerade / Until It's Time For You To Go / How? / That Old American Dream / Delta Dawn / You And Me Against The World / Leave Me Alone (Ruby Red Dress) / Crazy Love / The Old Fashioned Way / And I Love You So / A Song For You / The Westwind Circus / Hit The Road Jack / Stella By Starlight

Production Information:

Cover photography: Virgil Mirano

Notes / Trivia:

- This album contains material from 1971-1974.
- The album was released in Japan only in 1975 to tie in with Helen's tour there that year. The cover photograph appears on the back of the 1975 Japanese tour program.
- Album comes with a lyric / bio insert of 8 pages.
- Instead of a double LP set with 10 tracks per album, this is a single LP with 10 tracks per side. Volume of the songs had to be decreased during lacquer cutting to fit that material, but the sound, like all Japanese albums, is superb.

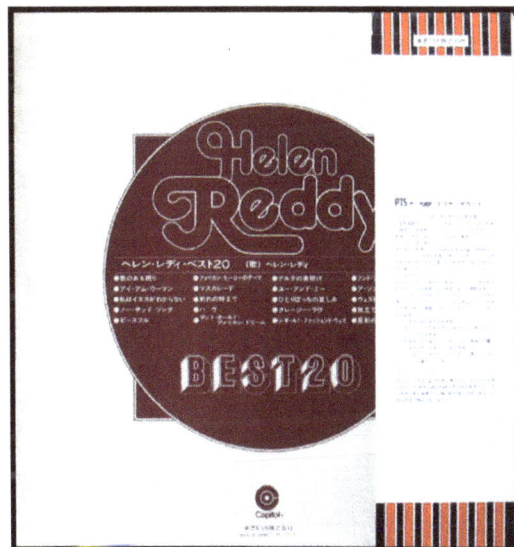

The back of the jacket.

The Best Of Helen Reddy
S22-18316

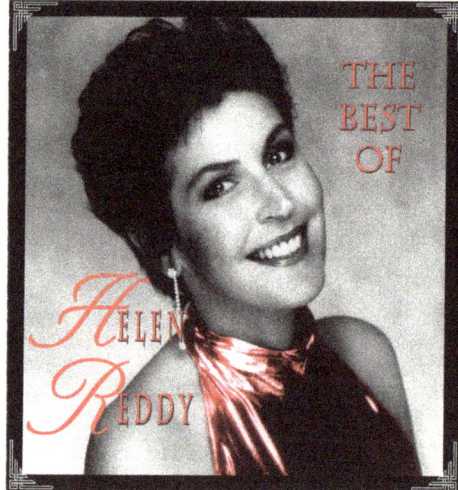

Track Listing:
Disc One:
I Am Woman / Leave Me Alone (Ruby Red Dress) / Ain't No Way To Treat A Lady / Keep On Singing / Somewhere In The Night / Free & Easy / We'll Sing In The Sunshine / Delta Dawn / Let Me Be Your Woman / Best Friend / A Song For You / You Make Me Feel So Young / You're My World / I Don't Know How To Love Him

Disc Two:
Peaceful / I Believe In Music / You And Me Against The World / Angie Baby / I Got A Name / Emotion / Bluebird / Candle On The Water / Crazy Love / Make Love To Me / Looks Like Love / Until It's Time For You To Go

Production Information:
Executive Producers: Steve Devick and Thomas R. Leavens
Compilation By: Thomas R. Leavens
Production Coordination: Maribeth Ackerman and Jill Highland
Art Direction / Design: Charles Macak Design
A Production of Staff Records

Notes / Trivia:

- A 1995 two CD set that is increasingly difficult to find.
- Comes in two separate CD cases, each with the same graphics. Was thought to have a cover box though the author's copy did not.
- Released by Staff Records in co-operation with CEMA Special Markets, a division of Capitol Records, Inc 1750 N. Vine Street Los Angeles, CA.

Come With Me – The Rest of Helen Reddy
HR-1002

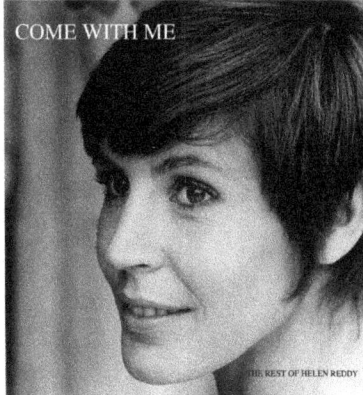

COME WITH ME
THE REST OF HELEN REDDY

1. Come With Me (previously unreleased)
2. Wonder Child
3. I Make Up Songs
4. Fool On The Hill
5. Never Say Goodbye
6. You're The One (duet with Tom Sullivan)
7. Little Boys (from The Man Who Loved Women)
8. Don't Throw It All Away
9. That's What Friends Are For
10. I Still Call Australia Home
11. Breezin' Along With The Breeze (duet with Toni Lamond)
12. I Am Woman (instrumental version)

Copyright © 2006 Helen Reddy Inc.

Track Listing:
1.) Come With Me (Written and recorded for the theme to "Women of the World" a shelved documentary TV series I created, produced and hosted in the early 1980's)
2.) Wonder Child (Recorded in 1979 for "The Stars Come Out on Sesame Street" LP)
3.) I Make Up Songs (Recorded in 1979 for "The Stars Come Out on Sesame Street" LP)
4.) Fool on the Hill (From "All This and World War II" – 1976)
5.) Never Say Goodbye (Theme from "Continental Divide" – 1981)
6.) You're The One (Duet with Tom Sullivan / Theme from "If You Could See What I Hear" – 1982)
7.) Little Boys (Ending theme from "The Man Who Loved Woman" – 1983)
8.) Don't Throw It All Away (Outtake from the "Imagination" LP 1982)
9.) That's What Friends Are For (Recorded for a Burt Bacharach tribute album in 1998)
10.) I Still Call Australia Home (Recorded in the early 90s for a program in Australia but never used)
11.) Breezin' Along With The Breeze (Duet with my sister Toni Lamond, from her "Still A Gypsy" CD 1999)
12.) I Am Woman (Instrumental – the backing track I used for live performances on television in the 1970's. Duplicated from the original master tape.)

Notes / Trivia:
- This is a CD that Helen released through her fan club in 2006 of what she called "A compilation of rare and unreleased songs." Song descriptions above are Helen's.
- You could buy each song separately or the complete CD, the author opted for the complete collection which arrived on a CD with printed label (below) and an email gave you a link to print the pdf of the cover above.

Play Me Out / Imagination

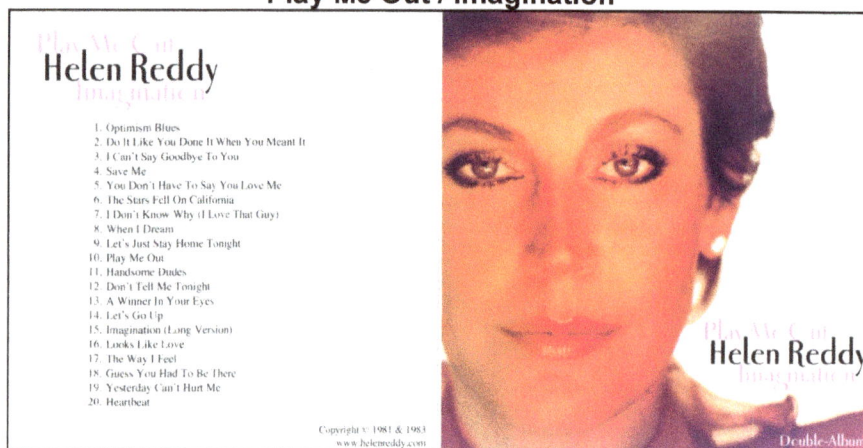

Track Listing:
Optimism Blues / Do It Like You Done It When You Meant It / I Can't Say Goodbye To You / Save Me / You Don't Have To Say You Love Me / The Stars Fell On California / I Don't Know Why (I Love That Guy) / When I Dream / Let's Just Stay Home Tonight / Play Me Out / Handsome Dudes / Don't Tell Me Tonight / A Winner In Your Eyes / Let's Go Up / Imagination (Long Version) / Looks Like Love / The Way I Feel / Guess You Had To Be There / Yesterday Can't Hurt Me / Heartbeat

Notes / Trivia:
- This was a project that Helen released through her fan club (www.helenreddy.com) sometime in the mid 2000's of her 1981 and 1983 MCA albums on a single disc. You would download the 20 song file and make your own CD or listen through your computer. I believe Helen owned the master tapes to these two early 1980's albums. A link was provided after purchase to download a hi-res cover as seen above.
- These two MCA albums and Helen's last two albums for Capitol, *Reddy* and *Take What You Find* are the only of her albums not to be released on compact disc.

Soundtracks

Pete's Dragon
SW-11704

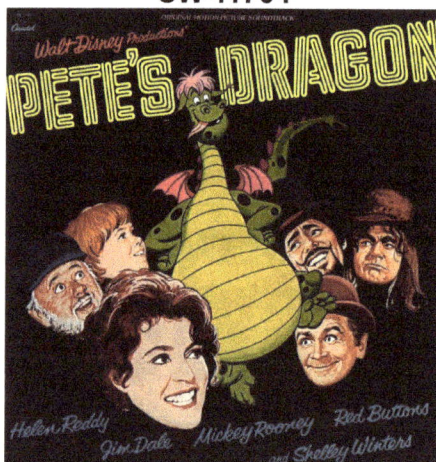

Track Listing:

Main Title / Candle On The Water (Helen Reddy) / I Saw A Dragon (Townsmen, Helen Reddy, Mickey Rooney) / It's Not Easy (Helen Reddy, Sean Marshall) / Every Little Piece (Jim Dale, Red Buttons) / The Happiest Home In These Hills (Charles Tyner, Gary Morgan, Jeff Conaway, Shelley Winters) / Brazzle Dazzle Day (Helen Reddy, Mickey Rooney, Sean Marshall) / Boo Bop BopBop Bop (I Love You, Too) (Charlie Callas, Sean Marshall) / There's Room For Everyone (Children, Helen Reddy, Sean Marshall) / Passamashloddy (Townsfolk, Jim Dale, Red Buttons) / Bill Of Sale (Charles Tyner, Gary Morgan, Helen Reddy, Jeff Conaway, Shelley Winters) / Candle On The Water (Reprise) (Helen Reddy)

Production Information:

Music and Lyrics By: Al Kasha /Joel Hirschhorn
Music Supervised, arrangements and Conductor by: Irwin Kostal
Mastered At: Capitol Mastering by: Ken Perry
Pressed By: Capitol Records Pressing Plant, Los Angeles, California, Capitol Records Pressing Plant, Jacksonville, Illinois and Capitol Records Pressing Plant, Winchester, Virginia.

Notes / Trivia:

- This album was released on LP, 8-Track and Cassette on 1977. The album was re-issued in 2002 on CD in the US and in 2006 in Europe with different artwork and graphics by Walt Disney Records.
- The LP pressings contained an inner LP photo sleeve with scenes from the film one on side and a full image of Helen singing "Candle On The Water" on the reverse.
- Merchandising included a metal lunch box, a Disney 7" record with 24 page storybook (#369) and was also available in a cassette tape version with same book (#19DC), a Disney "Story Teller" LP and book (Cat.# 3818), trading cards, comic books, coloring book, Colorforms set (# 624), GAF View-Master Reels, Little Golden Book, Tell-A-Tell Book (#2637), Golden Shape Book (#5891), Hand cranked movie viewer with cartridge, Newspaper Comic strips and various other items.
- The film has been issued on VHS Tape, CED, Laser Disc, DVD, Blu-ray and in 1977 a special 400 foot Super-8 reel of select scenes.
- The film was dubbed into many different languages for release around the world.
- Production started in July 1976 and wrapped in September 1976. Post production and looping began in October 1976.
- Music pre-recording took place several months in advance of filming.
- Reviews of the film were mixed.

The Man Who Loved Woman
VCL-1079

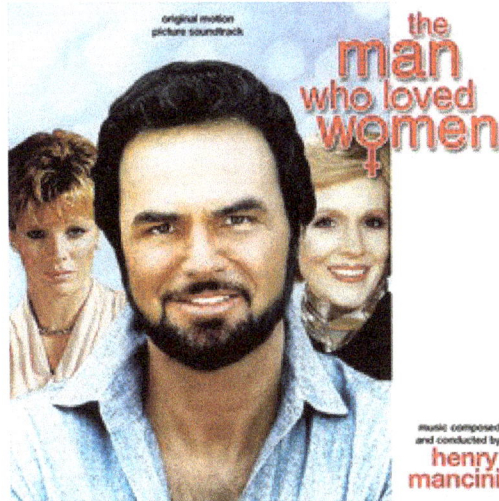

Track Listing:
Main Title / Meeting Agnes / F Minor Stretch / Locked Legs / David's Story / Blood and Bruises / Girls Paid For / Off to Houston / Welcome to Houston / Texas Barbecue / Lousie / The Little Doggy Waltz / Just Talk / One More Time / Market Music / Two on One / The Analyst Resigns / The Boat Ride / Tequila Sunrise / Tequila Sunset / Swan Lake (Tchaikovsky) / Blackie's Tune (Jazz Quartet) / God Rest Ye Merry Gentlemen / Deck the Halls / Gathering the Clan / The Funeral / Little Boys (End Title – Vocal: Helen Reddy) / Trailer / Meeting Agnes (alternate)

Production Information:
Music by: Henry Mancini / Pyotr Tchaikovsky
Lyrics by: Alan and Marilyn Bergman
Producers: Robert Townson / Henry Mancini
Editor: John C. Hammell
Mastering engineer: Erick Labson

Notes / Trivia:

- This CD was released as a Limited edition of 2000 copies on June 30, 2008.
- This soundtrack had never been released before.
- The film was released December 16, 1983.

The back of the CD case with Helen's name in blue bottom row of track credits.

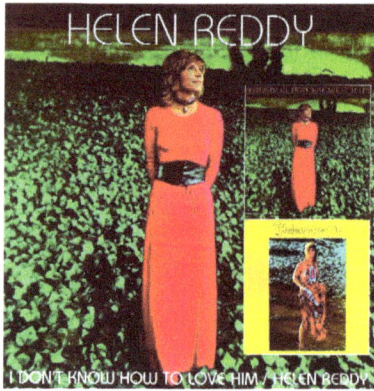

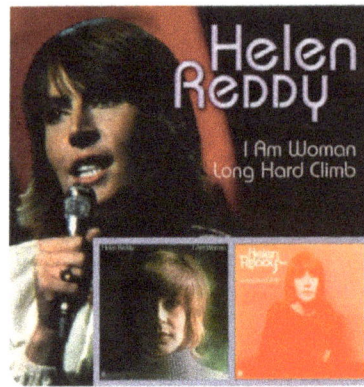

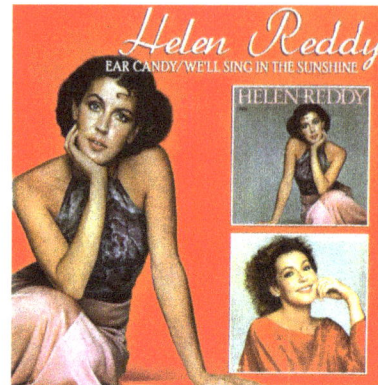

Specialty CD Releases

→

A majority of Helen's Capitol recordings have been officially licensed and released. The exceptions are her final two Capitol albums that have not been reissued on CD. Here are the best CD's to buy if you are looking for complete vintage Helen albums on CD and with *bonus material. Each disc had two albums on one disc.

Two-On-One Discs

I Don't Know How To Love Him / Helen Reddy (RVCD-211 / April 4, 2005)
Crazy Love / How Can I Be Sure / Our House / I Am Woman / L.A. Breakdown / A Song For You / Don't Make Promises / I Believe In Music / Best Friend / I Don't Know How To Love Him / Time / How? / Come On John / Summer of '71 / I Don't Remember My Childhood / No Sad Song / I Think It's Going To Rain Today / Tulsa Turnaround / More Than You Could Take / New Year's Resovolution / *Go (1968 Fontana recording) / *The Junkman's Serenade (1968 Fontana recording) / *Medley – (Live In London / May 1978): I Don't Know How To Love Him – I Believe In Music – Crazy Love

I Am Woman / Long Hard Climb (RVCD-168 / August 4, 2003)
Peaceful / I Am Woman / This Masquerade / I Didn't Mean To Love You / Where Is My Friend / And I Love You So / What Would They Say / Where Is The Love / Hit The Road Jack / The Last Blues Song / Leave Me Alone (Ruby Red Dress) / Lovin' You / A Bit Of OK / Don't Mess With A Woman / Delta Dawn / The West Wind Circus / If We Could Still Be Friends / Long Hard Climb / Until It's Time For You To Go / The Old Fashioned Way / *The West Wind Circus (Live In London / May 1978) / *This Masquerade (Live In London / May 1978)
(These two albums (minus the *bonus tracks) were also released recently on one SACD Hybrid Multi-channel "quad" format disc by Vocalion. The disc can be played on any regular CD player, but will playback in quad on a SACD player / CDLK4627)

Love Song For Jeffrey / Free And Easy (RVCD-170 / January 16, 2004)
That Old American Dream / You're My Home / Songs / I Got A Name / Keep On Singing / You And Me Against The World / Ah, My Sister / Pretty, Pretty / Love Song For Jeffrey / Stella By Starlight / Angie Baby / Raised On Rock / I've Been Wanting You So Long / You Have Lived / I'll Be Your Audience / Emotion (Amoreuse) / Free And Easy / Loneliness / Think I'll Write A Song / Showbiz (with The Pointer Sisters) / *Angie Baby (Live In London / May 1978) / *The Entertainer (Live In London / May 1978)

No Way To Treat A Lady / Music, Music (RVCD-212 / August 29, 2005)
Ain't No Way To Treat A Lady / Bluebird / Don't Let It Mess Your Mind / Somewhere In The Night / You Don't Need A Reason / Ten To Eight / Birthday Song / You Know Me / Nothing Good Comes Easy / Long Time Looking / Music, Music / Gladiola / Mama / Hold Me In Your Dreams / Get Off Me Baby / I Can't Hear You No More / Ladychain / Music Is My Life / Nice To Be Around / You Make It So Easy / *One Way Ticket (1968 Fontana recording)

Ear Candy / We'll Sing In The Sunshine (RVCD-312 / February 23, 2010)
You're My World / One More Night / Long Distance Love / If It's Magic / Aquarius Miracle / Laissez Les Bontemps Rouler / The Happy Girls / Midnight Skies / Baby, I'm A Star / Thank You / Ready Or Not / All I Ever Need / Poor Little Fool / One After 909 / I'd Rather Be Alone / Lady Of The Night / Catch My Breath / We'll Sing In The Sunshine / Blue / If I Ever Had To Say Goodbye To You

The Live Album

$\longrightarrow$

Live In London
SKBO-11873 / 2 LP Set

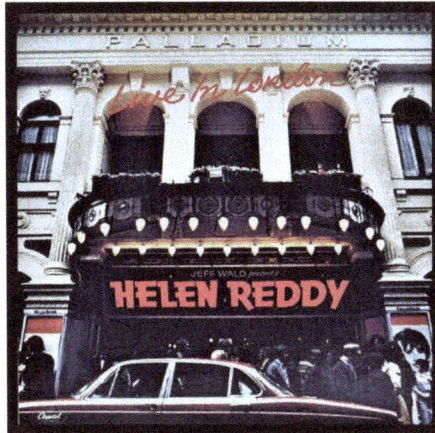

Track Listing:
Rhythm Rhapsody / This Masquerade / Bluebird / Candle on the Water (from *Pete's Dragon)* / Hold Me in Your Dreams Tonight / Angie Baby / Poor Little Fool / Ready or Not / The West Wind Circus / We'll Sing in the Sunshine / Mama / You're My World / I Can't Hear You No More / The Entertainer / Medley introduction - Medley: I Don't Know How to Love Him - I Believe in Music - Crazy Love - Peaceful - You and Me Against the World - Delta Dawn - Ain't No Way to Treat a Lady - Leave Me Alone (Ruby Red Dress) - The Last Blues Song - Keep On Singing - I Am Woman - I'll Be Your Audience

Production Information:
Produced by: John Palladino and Helen Reddy
Recorded at: London Palladium, London, England
Engineer: Doug Hopkins
Assistant Engineer: Jay Ranellucci
Mixed and Assembled at: Capitol Records, Hollywood, CA by David Cole
Cover Photography: Terry O'Neill
Art Direction: Roy Kohara
Production Management: Stephen Lewis
Public Relations: Linda Grey

Artist Management: Jeff Wald

Musicians:
Lead Guitar / Conductor / Orchestra Conductor: Lenny Coltun
Bass: Dave Parlato
Drums: Ron Tutt
Rhythm Guitar: Richie Zito
Piano: Tom Hensley / Helen Reddy on "Hold Me In Your Dreams Tonight"
Lead Trumpet: Ricky Baptist
And The Gordon Rose Orchestra
Background Vocals: Verna Richardson / Karin Patterson / Onike

Singles released from this album:
"Mama" b/w "The West Wind Circus" – October 30, 1978 (Cat. # 4654)

Notes / Trivia:
• The album was released on LP, Cassette, 8-Track and Open Reel Tape in December 1978.

- This album was recorded at Helen's three-night plus one Matinée appearance at the London Palladium on May 11,12 and 13, 1978.
- The release did not make any music charts.
- Released officially on CD by DRG on June 25, 2002 (DRGCD-91472)
- In the December 9, 1978 issue of Cash Box the reviewer writes: "Recorded at the Palladium in London, this double LP captures the sparkle and energy of this veteran songstress in concert. This package contains virtually all of her hit singles, most of which are presented in a lengthy medley on side four. Also featured on the LP are several capable renditions of such familiar tracks as "This Masquerade," "The Entertainer" and "Bluebird." Reddy's voice remains in top form throughout this album."
- In *Billboard*'s July 20, 2002 issue a review of the release of the album on compact disc under the "Vital Reissues" heading, Mitchell Paoletta says: "Ready for the flashback of a lifetime? If so, give a listen to *Live in London*, which has lost none of its sheen. Of course, a major part of its charm is its deliciously time-sensitive, disco-inflected orchestrations (the set was originally released by Capitol in 1978). While Reddy delivers the hits ("I Am Woman," among others), her classy renderings of Billy Joel's "The Entertainer" and Leon Russell's "This Masquerade" should not be overlooked.
- There was a budget single album version released also (Cat. No. SN-16250) that included only the first album of the two album set. Same graphics front and back, but no gate-fold.

The 8-Track tape cartridge was a big seller through the CRC!

The Singles

Helen Reddy Singles
PS- Picture Sleeve

1968

Go / Go – FDJ-9 (Fontana) / US / DJ Copy / Pink Label / Stereo-Mono
One Way Ticket / Go – F-1611 (Fontana) / US / DJ Copy / Blue Label
One Way Ticket / Go – F-1611 (Fontana) / US / Red Label / Plug Side
One Way Ticket / Go – BF-384 (Philips) / Australia (peaked at # 83 / ARIA Chart)

From what Helen told me, "Go," "One Way Ticket" and "The Junkman's Serenade" were all recorded in 1968 at the same three hour session in Chicago at Universal Recording months before she left to live in Los Angeles. "Go" and "One Way Ticket" were issued as a single (Cat. # F-1611). But I believe "The Junkman's Serenade" remained unreleased on vinyl until Pickwick issued the album "Helen Reddy / Shirley Bassey / Dusty Springfield" in 1973 once Helen really hit it big.

1971

I Don't Know How To Love Him / I Believe In Music – P-3027 (Capitol) / US / Promo
I Don't Know How To Love Him / I Believe In Music – 3027 (Capitol) / US
I Don't Know How To Love Him / I Believe In Music – 3027 (Capitol) / Canada
I Don't Know How To Love Him / I Believe In Music – 1C 006-80-767 U (Capitol) / Germany / PS
I Don't Know How To Love Him / I Believe In Music – 5C 006-80767 (Capitol) / Netherlands / Black Label / PS
I Don't Know How To Love Him / I Believe In Music – 5C 006-80767 (Capitol) / Netherlands / Orange Label / PS
I Don't Know How To Love Him / I Believe In Music – CP-9400 (Capitol) / Australia
I Don't Know How To Love Him / I Believe In Music – F.3027 (Capitol) / New Zealand
I Don't Know How To Love Him / I Believe In Music – CL-15679 (Capitol) / Norway / PS
I Don't Know How To Love Him / I Believe In Music – CL-15679 (Capitol) / Sweden / PS
I Don't Know How To Love Him / I Believe In Music – SN-20.568 (Capitol) / Spain / PS
I Don't Know How To Love Him / I Believe In Music – CL-15679 (Capitol) / UK
I Don't Know How To Love Him / I Believe In Music – CL-15729 (Capitol) / UK / Promo
I Don't Know How To Love Him / I Believe In Music – CL-15715 (Capitol) / UK / Re-issue / Promo
I Don't Know How To Love Him / I Believe In Music – CR-2808 (Capitol) / Japan / PS

La Chanson De Marie-Madeleine (I Don't Know How To Love Him) / Crazy Love – 2C 006-80.922M (Capitol) / France / PS

I Don't Know How To Love Him - I Believe In Music (Helen Reddy) / Long Cool Woman - Cable Car (The Hollies) – 11137 (S) / Thailand / 7", 45 RPM, EP / PS / Probable bootleg

Crazy Love / Crazy Love – 3138 (Capitol) / US / DJ Copy / Stereo-Mono
Crazy Love / Best Friend – 3138 (Capitol) / US
Crazy Love / Best Friend – 3138 (Capitol) / Canada
Crazy Love / Best Friend – P-3138 (Capitol) / Canada / DJ Copy
Crazy Love / Best Friend – F.3138 (Capitol) / New Zealand
Crazy Love / Best Friend – CR-2885 (Capitol) / Japan / PS
Crazy Love / Best Friend – 76384 (Capitol) / US / Acetate

Crazy Love / Our House – CP-9607 (Capitol) / Australia

1972

Summer of '71 / I Think It's Going To Rain Today – CP554 (Capitol) / New Zealand

No Sad Song / No Sad Song – PRO-6363 (Capitol) (US) / DJ Copy / Stereo-Mono
No Sad Song / More Than You Could Take – 3231 (Capitol) / US
No Sad Song / More Than You Could Take – 3231 (Capitol) / Canada
No Sad Song / More Than You Could Take – CL 15706 (Capitol) / UK
No Sad Song / More Than You Could Take – 5C 006-81019 (Capitol) / Netherlands / PS
No Sad Song / More Than You Could Take – 3C 006-81019 (Capitol) / Italy / PS
No Sad Song / More Than You Could Take – 5E 006-81019 (Capitol) / Finland
No Sad Song / More Than You Could Take – 4E 006-81019 (Capitol) / Sweden / PS
No Sad Song / More Than You Could Take – 7E 006-81019 (Capitol) / Norway
Plus De Chansons Tristes (No Sad Song) / Summer of '71 – 2 C006-81100 (Capitol) / France / PS
No Sad Song / More Than You Could Take – 1C 006-81 019 (Capitol) / Germany / PS
No Sad Song / More Than You Could Take – CP-9757 (Capitol) / Australia
No Sad Song / More Than You Could Take – 2C 006-81019 (Capitol) / France / PS
No Sad Song / More Than You Could Take – CR-2971 (Capitol) / Japan / PS

*I Am Woman / Summer of '71 – CL 15721 (Capitol) / UK
*I Am Woman / Summer of '71 – CL 15721 (Capitol) / UK / PS / Promo
*I Am Woman / Summer of '71 – CL 15721 (Capitol) / Greece
*I Am Woman / Summer of '71 – 3C 006-81171 (Capitol) / Italy
*I Am Woman / Summer of '71 – 1 C 006-81171 M (Capitol) / Germany / PS
*I Am Woman / Summer of '71 – 5C 006-81171 (Capitol) / Netherlands / PS

*I Am Woman / Come On John – 2 C006 - 81185 (Capitol) / France / PS

*Original Larry Marks 2:15 version as recorded at A&M Recording in Los Angeles and appearing on Helen's first album "I Don't Know How To Love Him." (1971 / ST-762).

+I Am Woman / I Am Woman – P-3350 (Capitol) / (US) / DJ Copy / Stereo-Mono
+I Am Woman / More Than You Could Take – 3350 (Capitol) / US
+I Am Woman / More Than You Could Take – 3350 (Capitol) / Canada
+I Am Woman / More Than You Could Take – CP-9953 (Capitol) / Australia
+I Am Woman / More Than You Could Take – SN-20.700 (Capitol) / Spain / PS
+I Am Woman / More Than You Could Take – JCL 522 (Capitol) / South Africa
+I Am Woman / More Than You Could Take – SP 20 053 (Capitol) / Portugal / PS
+I Am Woman / More Than You Could Take – ECR-10210 (Capitol) / Japan / PS / Translucent Red Vinyl

+The Jay Senter 3:04 re-recorded version with the added verse recorded April 23, 1972 at SunWest Studios in Hollywood and appearing on Helen's third album "I Am Woman" (1972 / ST-11068). More information on the re-recorded version at the end of the single section.

Peaceful / Peaceful – P-3527 (Capitol) (US) / DJ Copy / White Label / Stereo-Mono
Peaceful / What Would They Say – 3527 (Capitol) / US
Peaceful / What Would They Say – 3527 (Capitol) / Canada
Peaceful / What Would They Say – 7E 006-81374 (Capitol) / Norway
Peaceful / What Would They Say – F. 3527 (Capitol) / New Zealand
Peaceful / What Would They Say – 6E 006-81374 (Capitol) / Denmark / PS
Peaceful / What Would They Say – SP-20.109 (Capitol) / Portugal / PS
Peaceful / What Would They Say – 5C 006-81374 (Capitol) / Netherlands / PS

Peaceful / What Would They Say – CP-10137 (Capitol) / Australia

Peaceful / The Last Blues Song – CL 15745 (Capitol) / UK / DJ Copy

I Am Woman / More Than You Could Take / Peaceful / What Would They Say – CAP 39201 (Capitol) EP / Chile / PS

1973

Peaceful / What Would They Say – 1C 006-81 374 (Capitol / EMI) / Germany / PS
Peaceful / What Would They Say – SN-20754 (Capitol / Movie-Play) / Spain / PS

Delta Dawn / Delta Dawn – P-3645 (Capitol) / US / DJ Copy
Delta Dawn / If We Could Still Be Friends – 3645 (Capitol) / US
Delta Dawn / If We Could Still Be Friends – 3645 (Capitol) / Canada
Delta Dawn / If We Could Still Be Friends – SN-20.804 (Capitol / Movie Play) / Spain / PS
Delta Dawn / If We Could Still Be Friends – 2C 006-81.462 (Capitol) / France / PS
Delta Dawn / If We Could Still Be Friends – ECR-10411 (Capitol) / Japan / PS
Delta Dawn / If We Could Still Be Friends – CP-10257 (Capitol) / Australia
Delta Dawn / If We Could Still Be Friends – F.3645 (Capitol) / New Zealand
Delta Dawn / If We Could Still Be Friends – 5C 006-81462 (Capitol) / Netherlands / PS
Delta Dawn / If We Could Still Be Friends – 5C 006-81462 (Capitol) / Italy / PS
Delta Dawn / If We Could Still Be Friends – 5C 006-81462 (Capitol) / Sweden / PS
Delta Dawn / If We Could Still Be Friends – CL-P 15757 (Capitol) / UK / Promo
Delta Dawn / If We Could Still Be Friends – CL 15757 (Capitol) / UK
Delta Dawn / If We Could Still Be Friends – 1C 006-81 462 (Capitol / EMI) / Germany / PS

Leave Me Alone (Ruby Red Dress) / Leave Me Alone (Ruby Red Dress) / P-3768 (Capitol) / US / DJ Copy / White-Label / Stereo-Mono
Leave Me Alone (Ruby Red Dress) / The Old Fashioned Way – 3768 (Capitol) / US
Leave Me Alone (Ruby Red Dress) / The Old Fashioned Way – 3768 (Capitol) / Canada
Leave Me Alone (Ruby Red Dress) / The Old Fashioned Way – CL 15770 (Capitol) / UK / PS
Leave Me Alone (Ruby Red Dress) / The Old Fashioned Way – CL 15770 (Capitol) / UK / Promo
Leave Me Alone (Ruby Red Dress) / The Old Fashioned Way – 5C 006-81551 (Capitol / EMI) / Netherlands / PS / Includes a clipable Jukebox strip on the backside.
Leave Me Alone (Ruby Red Dress) / The Old Fashioned Way – 1C 006-81 551 (Capitol / EMI) / Germany / PS
Leave Me Alone (Ruby Red Dress) / The Old Fashioned Way – F.3768 (Capitol) / New Zealand

Leave Me Alone (Ruby Red Dress) / Don't Mess With A Woman – CP-10342 (Capitol) / Australia

1974

Leave Me Alone (Ruby Red Dress) / The Old Fashioned Way – SN-20861 (Capitol / Movie Play) / Spain / PS

Keep On Singing / Keep On Singing – P-3845 (Capitol) / US / DJ Copy / White Label / Stereo-Mono
Keep On Singing / You're My Home – 3845 (Capitol) / US
Keep On Singing / You're My Home – 3845 (Capitol) / Canada
Keep On Singing / You're My Home – CL 15782 (Capitol) / UK
Keep On Singing / You're My Home – CP10450 (Capitol) / Australia
Keep On Singing / You're My Home – F.3845 (Capitol) / New Zealand
Keep On Singing / You're My Home – SN-20.900 (Capitol / Movie Play) / Spain / PS

Keep On Singing / You're My Home – 1C006 81623 (Capitol / EMI) / Germany / PS
Keep On Singing / You're My Home – 5C 006-81623 (Capitol / EMI) / Netherlands / PS
Keep On Singing / You're My Home – 4E 006-81623 (Capitol) / Sweden / PS
Keep On Singing / You're My Home – ECR-10524 (Capitol) / Japan / PS
Keep On Singing / You're My Home – 2C 008-81.623 (Capitol) / France / PS

That Old American Dream / Love Song For Jeffrey – 1C 006-81677 (Capitol / EMI) / Germany / PS

You And Me Against The World / You And Me Against The World – P-3897 (Capitol) / US / DJ Copy / White Label / Stereo-Mono
You And Me Against The World / Love Song For Jeffrey– 3897 (Capitol) / US
You And Me Against The World / Love Song For Jeffrey– 3897 (Capitol) / Canada
You And Me Against The World / Love Song For Jeffrey– CL-15788 (Capitol) / UK
You And Me Against The World / Love Song For Jeffrey– ECR-10558 (Capitol) / Japan / PS
You And Me Against The World / Love Song For Jeffrey– CP-10516 (Capitol) / Australia
You And Me Against The World / Love Song For Jeffrey– F.3897 (Capitol) / New Zealand

Angie Baby / Angie Baby – 3972 (Capitol) / US / DJ Copy / White Label / Stereo-Mono
Angie Baby / Think I'll Write A Song – 3972 (Capitol) / US
Angie Baby / Think I'll Write A Song – 3972 (Capitol) / Canada
Angie Baby / Think I'll Write A Song – CL 15799 (Capitol) / UK
Angie Baby / Think I'll Write A Song – 006-81 782 (Capitol) / Finland
Angie Baby / Think I'll Write A Song – SN-20.942 (Capitol / Movie Play) / Spain / PS
Angie Baby / Think I'll Write A Song – 1C 006-81 782 (Capitol / EMI) / Germany / PS
Angie Baby / Think I'll Write A Song – F.3972 (Capitol) / New Zealand
Angie Baby / Think I'll Write A Song – ECR-10653 (Capitol) / Japan / PS
Angie Baby / Think I'll Write A Song – CP-10645 (Capitol) / Australia
Angie Baby / Think I'll Write A Song – CL 15799 (Capitol) / Ireland
Angie Baby / Think I'll Write A Song – 2C 004-81.782 (Capitol) / France / PS
Angie Baby / Think I'll Write A Song – 5C 006-81782 (Capitol) / Netherlands / PS
Angie Baby / Think I'll Write A Song – 5E 006-81782 (Capitol) / Finand

Emotion / Emotion – 4021 (Capitol) / US / DJ Copy / White Label / Stereo-Mono
Emotion / I've Been Wanting You So Long – 4021 (Capitol) / US
Emotion / I've Been Wanting You So Long – 4021 (Capitol) / Canada
Emotion / I've Been Wanting You So Long – ECR-10717 (Capitol) / Japan / PS
Emotion / I've Been Wanting You So Long – SN-20.992 (Capitol / Movie Play) / Spain / PS

This 1974 single above (#4021) is an oddity. The only consumer stereo copy I could find was the 1984 reissue on Starline. However there was a promo issue released in Stereo-Mono and I believe the Japanese release is stereo. The album cut is in stereo however.

Free and Easy / I've Been Wanting You So Long – CP-10766 (Capitol) / Australia
Free and Easy / I've Been Wanting You So Long – CP-590 (Capitol) / New Zealand

1975

I Am Woman / Free And Easy – CL 15815 (Capitol) / UK
I Am Woman / Free And Easy – CL 15815 (Capitol) / Ireland

Angie Baby – R-0676 (TonPress) / Poland / Flexi-disc, 6" 45 RPM / Mono / Single-Sided / Various photos used on backing card, none of Helen herself.

Best Friend / Crazy Love ECR-10664 (Capitol) Japan / PS / Japanese single for the film "Airport 1975"

You Don't Need A Reason / You Don't Need A Reason – P-4098 (Capitol) / US / DJ Copy / White Label / Stereo-Mono

Bluebird / Bluebird – P-4108 (Capitol) / US / DJ Copy / White Label / Stereo-Mono
Bluebird / You Don't Need A Reason – 4108 (Capitol) / US
Bluebird / You Don't Need A Reason – 4108 (Capitol) / Canada
Bluebird / You Don't Need A Reason – ECR-10795 (Capitol) / Japan / PS
Bluebird / You Don't Need A Reason – F.4108 (Capitol) / New Zealand
Bluebird / You Don't Need A Reason – CL 15829 (Capitol) / UK

Ain't No Way To Treat A Lady / Ain't No Way To Treat A Lady – P-4128 (Capitol) / US /DJ Copy / White Label / Stereo-Mono
Ain't No Way To Treat A Lady / Long Time Looking – 4128 (Capitol) / US
Ain't No Way To Treat A Lady / Long Time Looking – 4128 (Capitol) / Canada
Ain't No Way To Treat A Lady / Long Time Looking – 1C 006-81 984 (Capitol / EMI) / Germany / PS
Ain't No Way To Treat A Lady / Long Time Looking – 5C 006-81984 (Capitol) / Netherlands / PS
No Es Manera de Tratar A Una Dama (Ain't No Way To Treat A Lady) / (Mirando Por Mucho Tiempo) Long Time Looking – 4128 (Capitol) / Guatemala
Ain't No Way To Treat A Lady / Long Time Looking – CL 15835 (Capitol) / UK
Ain't No Way To Treat A Lady / Long Time Looking – 3C 006 81984 (Capitol / Odeon) / Italy
Ain't No Way To Treat A Lady / Long Time Looking – CP-10910 (Capitol) / Australia
Ain't No Way To Treat A Lady / Long Time Looking – F.4128 (Capitol) / New Zealand
Ain't No Way To Treat A Lady / Long Time Looking – ECR-10852 (Capitol) / Japan / PS

Somewhere In The Night / Somewhere In The Night – P-4192 (Capitol) / US / DJ Copy / White Label / Stereo-Mono
Somewhere In The Night / Ten To Eight – 4192 (Capitol) / US
Somewhere In The Night / Ten To Eight – 4192 (Capitol) / Canada
Algún Lugar En La Noche (Somewhere In The Night) / Ocho Menos Diez (Ten To Eight) – 1440 (Capitol) / Argentina
Somewhere In The Night / Ten To Eight – CP-11033 (Capitol) / Australia
Somewhere In The Night / Ten To Eight – 3C 006 82095 (Capitol) / Italy / PS
Somewhere In The Night / Ten To Eight – ECR-10896 (Capitol) / Japan / PS

1976

No Es Manera De Tratar A Una Dama (Ain't No Way To Treat A Lady) / Emocion (Emotion) – 7884 (Capitol) / Mexico / PS

Hold Me In Your Dreams Tonight / You Make It So Easy – CL 15893 (Capitol) / UK / Marked: "Demo Record Not For Sale"

I Can't Hear You No More / I Can't Hear You No More – 4312 (Capitol) / US / DJ Copy / White Label / Stereo-Mono
I Can't Hear You No More / Music Is My Life – 4312 (Capitol) / US
I Can't Hear You No More / Music Is My Life – 4312 (Capitol) / Canada
I Can't Hear You No More / Music Is My Life – 5C 006-82300 (Capitol) / Netherlands / PS
No Puedo Escucharte Mas (I Can't Hear You No More) / La Musica Es MI Vida (Music Is My Life) – 4312 (Capitol) / Guatemala
I Can't Hear You No More / Music Is My Life – 1C 006-82 300 (Capitol) / Germany / PS
I Can't Hear You No More / Music Is My Life – ECR-20077 (Capitol) / Japan / PS

No Puedo Oirte Mas (I Can't Hear You No More) / La Musica Es MI Vida (Music Is My Life) – 7976 (Capitol) / Spain / PS
I Can't Hear You No More / Music Is My Life – CL 15883 (Capitol) / UK / Marked: "Demo Record Not For Sale"

Music, Music / Ladychain – ECR-20166 (Capitol) / Japan / PS / White Label Promotional Copy
Music, Music / Ladychain – ECR-20166 (Capitol) / Japan / PS

Gladiola / Gladiola – P-4350 (Capitol) / US / DJ Copy / White Label / Stereo-Mono
Gladiola / You Make It So Easy – 4350 (Capitol) / US
Gladiola / You Make It So Easy – 4350 (Capitol) / Canada
Gladiola / You Make It So Easy – CP-11296 (Capitol) / Australia

1977

You're My World / You're My World – P-4418 (Capitol) / US / DJ Copy / White Label / Stereo-Mono
You're My World / You're My World – P-4418 - PRO-8617 (Capitol) / Canada / DJ Copy / White Label / Stereo-Mono
You're My World / Thank You – 4418 (Capitol) / US
You're My World / Thank You – 4418 (Capitol) / Canada
Tu Eres Mi Mundo (You're My World) / Gracias (Thank You) – 4418 (Capitol) / Guatemala
You're My World / Thank You – ECR-20269 (Capitol) / Japan / PS
Eres Mi Mundo (You're My World) / Gracias (Thank You) – (Capitol) / Mexico
You're My World / Thank You – F.4418 (Capitol) / New Zealand
En Mi Mundo (You're My World) / Gracias (Thank You) – 1303 (Capitol / Odeon) / Chile
You're My World / Thank You – 3C 006 85167 (Capitol) / Italy / PS
You're My World / Thank You – 01 03 1036 (Capitol) / Peru

You're My World / Un Soldino – 3C 000-70112 (Capitol / EMI) / Italy / Helen on a the A side and an uncredited singer on the flip side / White Label

The Happy Girls / The Happy Girls – SPRO-8720 (Capitol) / US / DJ Copy / White Label / Stereo-Mono
The Happy Girls / The Happy Girls – P-4487 (Capitol) / US / DJ Copy / White Label / Stereo-Mono
The Happy Girls / The Happy Girls – P-4487 (Capitol) / Canada / DJ Copy / White Label / Stereo-Mono
The Happy Girls / Laissez Les Bontemps Rouler – CL 15948 (Capitol) / UK

Laissez Les Bontemps Rouler / Laissez Les Bontemps Rouler – 4487 (Capitol) / US / DJ Copy / White Label / Stereo-Mono
Laissez Les Bontemps Rouler / The Happy Girls – 4487 (Capitol) / US
Laissez Les Bontemps Rouler / The Happy Girls – 4487 (Capitol) / Canada

Long Distance Love / You're My World – CL 15927 (Capitol) / UK / PS
Long Distance Love / You're My World – CL 15927 (Capitol) / UK / PS / Marked: Demo Record Not For Sale
Long Distance Love / You're My World – CL 11490 (Capitol) / Australia

Candle On The Water / It's Not Easy / Brazzle Dazzle Day / There's Room For Everyone – DIS 15 – SPSR 432 (Disneyland / EMI) / UK / Marked: Demo Record Not For Sale / For Theatre Non-sync Use / Songs from Disney's Pete's Dragon Soundtrack

Candle on the Water / Candle on the Water – P-4521 (Capitol) / US / DJ Copy / White Label / Stereo-

Mono
Candle on the Water / Candle on the Water – PROMO-4521 (Capitol) / Canada / DJ Copy / White Label / Stereo-Mono
Candle on the Water / Brazzle Dazzle Day – 4521 (Capitol) / US / PS
Candle on the Water / Brazzle Dazzle Day – 4521 (Capitol) / Canada
Candle on the Water / Brazzle Dazzle Day – CP-11659 (Capitol) / Australia
Candle on the Water / Brazzle Dazzle Day – F.4521 (Capitol) / New Zealand

Note: This Capitol single above contains a different version of *Candle On The Water* than the one used in the film.

Midnight Skies / Long Distance Love – 5C 006-85 175 (Capitol) / Netherlands / PS

Baby, I'm A Star / Laissez Les Bontemps Rouler – 2C00685160 (Capitol) / France / PS

1978

You're My World (Helen Reddy) / Milk Shake Disco (Milk Shake) – R-0623-II (TonPress) / Poland / Flexi-disc, 6" 45 RPM / Mono / Single-Sided / Various photos used on backing card, none of Helen herself.

We'll Sing In The Sunshine / We'll Sing In The Sunshine – P-4555 (Capitol) / US / DJ Copy / Purple Label / Stereo-Mono
We'll Sing In The Sunshine / I'd Rather Be Alone – 4555 (Capitol) / US
We'll Sing In The Sunshine / I'd Rather Be Alone – 4555 (Capitol) / Canada
We'll Sing In The Sunshine / I'd Rather Be Alone – 3C 006 85507 (Capitol) / Italy / PS
We'll Sing In The Sunshine / I'd Rather Be Alone – ECR-20422 (Capitol) / Japan / PS
We'll Sing In The Sunshine / I'd Rather Be Alone – CP-11734 (Capitol) / Australia
We'll Sing In The Sunshine / I'd Rather Be Alone – F.4555 (Capitol) / New Zealand

Ready or Not / Ready or Not – P-4582 (Capitol) / US / DJ Copy / White Label / Stereo-Mono
Ready or Not / If I Ever Had To Say Goodbye to You – 4582 Capitol) / US
Ready or Not / If I Ever Had To Say Goodbye to You – 4582 (Capitol) / Canada
Ready or Not / One After 909 – CL 15984 (Capitol) / UK

Poor Little Fool / We'll Sing In The Sunshine – CL 16007 (Capitol) / UK

Mama / Mama – P-4654 (Capitol) / US / From the album "Live In London" / DJ Copy / White Label / Stereo-Mono
Mama / Mama – PROMO-4654 (Capitol) / Canada / From the album "Live In London" / DJ Copy / White Label / Stereo-Mono
Mama / West Wind Circus – 4654 (Capitol) / US / From the album "Live In London"

1979

Make Love To Me / Make Love To Me – P-4712 (Capitol) US / DJ Copy / White Label / Stereo-Mono
Make Love To Me / Make Love To Me – PRO-9092 (Capitol) / Canada / DJ Copy / White Label / Stereo-Mono
Make Love To Me / More Than You Could Take – 4712 (Capitol) / US
Make Love To Me / More Than You Could Take – 1 C 006-85 920 (Capitol / EMI) / Germany / PS
Make Love To Me / More Than You Could Take – CL 16089 (Capitol) / UK
Make Love To Me / Words Are Not Enough – CP-11997 (Capitol) / Australia
Make Love To Me / More Than You Could Take – 8517 (Capitol) / US / 12" Single

Make Love To Me / More Than You Could Take – 75018 (Capitol) / Canada / 12" Single
Make Love To Me / You're So Good – 1 C 052-85 955 (Capitol) / Germany / 12" Single / PS
Make Love To Me / Make Love To Me – SPRO-9117 (Capitol) US / DJ Copy / 12" Single / Yellow Translucent Vinyl

Wonder Child / I Make Up Songs – CTW-199073 (Sesame Street Records) US / PS – From the LP *The Stars Come Out On Sesame Street* (CTW-79007)

Let Me Be Your Woman / Let Me Be Your Woman – P-4786 (Capitol) / US / DJ Copy / White Label / Stereo-Mono
Let Me Be Your Woman / Let Me Be Your Woman – PRO-4786 (Capitol) / US / DJ Copy / White Label / Stereo-Mono
Let Me Be Your Woman / Trying To Get To You – 4786 (Capitol) / US
Let Me Be Your Woman / Trying To Get To You – 4786 (Capitol) / Canada

Minute by Minute / The Magic Is Still There – CP-11936 (Capitol) / Australia

1980

Take What You Find / Take What You Find – P-4867 (Capitol) / US / DJ Copy / White Label / Stereo-Mono
Take What You Find / Love's Not The Question – 4867 (Capitol) / US
Take What You Find / Love's Not The Question – 4867 (Capitol) / Canada
Take What You Find / Love's Not The Question – 1C 006-86 162 (Capitol) / Germany / PS
Take What You Find / Love's Not The Question – 1C 006-86 162 (Capitol) / Netherlands / PS
Take What You Find / Love's Not The Question – CL 16147 (Capitol) / UK / Marked: "Demo Record Not For Sale"
Take What You Find / Love's Not The Question – CL 16147 (Capitol) / UK
Take What You Find / Love's Not The Question – CP-265 (Capitol / EMI) / Australia
Take What You Find / Love's Not The Question – ECS-17021 (Capitol) / Japan / PS
Coge Lo Que Encuentres (Take What You Find) / Amor No Es La Cuestion (Love's Not The Question) – 10C 006-086162 (Capitol / EMI / Odeon) / Spain / PS

Take What You Find / Take What You Find – SPRO-9382 (Capitol) / US / 12" Promo Single

Take What You Find / Love's Not The Question / Take What You Find – 12CL 16147 (Capitol) / UK / 12" Extended Single

Killer Barracuda / A Way With The Ladies – 4918 (Capitol) / US
Killer Barracuda / A Way With The Ladies – 4918 (Capitol) / Canada

1981

I Can't Say Goodbye To You / I Can't Say Goodbye To You – MCA-51106 (MCA) / US / DJ Copy / White Label / Stereo-Mono
I Can't Say Goodbye To You / Let's Just Stay Home Tonight – MCA-51106 (MCA) / US
I Can't Say Goodbye To You / Let's Just Stay Home Tonight – MCA-51106 (MCA) / Canada
I Can't Say Goodbye To You / Let's Just Stay Home Tonight – MCA-51106 (MCA) / Australia
I Can't Say Goodbye To You / Let's Just Stay Home Tonight – VIMX-1523 (MCA) / Japan / PS
I Can't Say Goodbye To You / Save Me – MCA-744 (MCA) / UK / PS
I Can't Say Goodbye To You / Save Me – MCA-744 (MCA) / Ireland
I Can't Say Goodbye To You / Let's Just Stay Home Tonight – 103 267 (MCA) / France / PS
I Can't Say Goodbye To You / Let's Just Stay Home Tonight – 103.267 (MCA) / Netherlands / PS

I Can't Say Goodbye To You / Let's Just Stay Home Tonight – 103.267 (MCA) / Brazil / PS
Save Me / I Can't Say Goodbye To You – MSAM 717 (MCA) / UK

You Don't Have To Say You Love Me / The Stars Fell On California – VIMX-1529 (MCA) / Japan / PS

Theme From "Continental Divide" (Never Say Goodbye) / Theme From "Continental Divide" (Never Say Goodbye) – MCA-51186 (MCA) / US / DJ Copy / White Label / Stereo-Mono
Theme From "Continental Divide" (Never Say Goodbye) / When I Dream – MCA-51186 (MCA) / US
Theme From "Continental Divide" (Never Say Goodbye) / When I Dream – VIMX-1535 (MCA) / Japan / PS

1983

Don't Tell Me Tonight / Don't Tell Me Tonight – MCA-52170 (MCA) / DJ Copy / White Label / Stereo-Mono / Marked: Promotion Copy Not For Sale
Don't Tell Me Tonight / Yesterday Can't Hurt Me – MCA-52170 (MCA) / US / PS

Looks Like Love / Yesterday Can't Hurt Me – MCA-809 (MCA) / UK / PS

Imagination / Handsome Dudes – MCA-52209 (MCA) / Canada

Imagination / The Way I Feel – MCA-52221 (MCA) / US
Imagination / The Way I Feel – 105.325 (MCA) / Europe / PS
Imagination (Edited Version) / The Way I Feel – MCA-818 (MCA) / UK / PS
Imagination / The Way I Feel – MCAT-818 (MCA) / Europe / White Label Promo
Imagination (Special Extended Remix) / The Way I Feel – MCAT-818 (MCA) / Europe / 12" Single / MCA Disco Sleeve

Imagination (Extended Version) / Imagination – MCA-13964 (MCA) / US / 12" Single / PS
Imagination (Extended Version) / Imagination – MCA-13964 (MCA) / Canada / 12" Single / PS

1984

Imagination / Don't Tell Me Tonight – ZS-1207 (Wizard) / Australia
Imagination / Don't Tell Me Tonight – ZS-1207 (Wizard) / New Zealand

1993

Leave Me Alone (Ruby Red Dress) / I Don't Know How To Love Him – COL 6106 (CEMA Reissue) / US / Blue Label
Leave Me Alone (Ruby Red Dress) / I Don't Know How To Love Him – COL 6106 (CEMA Reissue) / US / Black Label

Angie Baby / You And Me Against The World – COL6107 (CEMA Reissue) / US / Blue Label
Angie Baby / You And Me Against The World – COL6107 (CEMA Reissue) / US / Black Label

I Am Woman / Delta Dawn – COL6129 (CEMA Reissue) / US / Blue Label
I Am Woman / Delta Dawn – COL6129 (CEMA Reissue) / US / Black Label

1994

Ain't No Way To Treat A Lady / You're My World – COL6353 (CEMA Reissue) / US / Blue Label
Ain't No Way To Treat A Lady / You're My World – COL6353 (CEMA Reissue) / US / Black Label

Ain't No Way To Treat A Lady / You're My World – COL6353 (CEMA Reissue) / US / Pink Label

1998

Surrender (The Remix) / Surrender (Album Version) – VS12-5818 (Varèse Sarabande) / US /12", 33 ⅓ RPM / Black sleeve with photo sticker

Surrender (The Remix) / Surrender (Album Version) – VSDS-5818 (Varèse Sarabande) / US / CD Maxi-Single / Full color insert

1970's / 1980's / Reissues

I Am Woman / I Don't Know How To Love Him – 6213 (Capitol / Starline Reissue) / US / Side 1 was originally released May 1972 and Side 2 was originally released January 1971

Peaceful / Delta Dawn - 6214 (Capitol / Starline Reissue) / US / Side 1 was originally released January 1973 and Side 2 was originally released June 1973

Leave Me Alone (Ruby Red Dress) / Ain't No Way To Treat A Lady – 6238 (Capitol / Starline Reissue) / US / Side 1 was originally released October 1973 and Side 2 was originally released August 1975

You And Me Against The World / Somewhere In The Night – X-6239 (Capitol / Starline Reissue) / US / Side 1 was originally released May 1974 and Side 2 was originally released November 1975

Angie Baby / Emotion – 6240 (Capitol Starline Reissue) / US / Side 1 was originally released October 1974 and Side 2 was originally released January 1975

You're My World / The Happy Girls – 6251 (Capitol Starline Reissue) / US / Side 1 originally released April 1977 and Side 2 was originally released September 1977

Unknown Release Years:

Side A: "Getaway" Instrumental Version by Bob Young & His Orchestra / Side B: "Getaway" Vocal: Helen Reddy – NZ-2171 (Consulate) / Rothmans Of Pallmall (AUST.) LTD. RECORDS AUSTRALIA (Likely mid-1960's) Possibly the first vinyl record pressed of Helen.

Patience & Prudence - Tonight You Belong To Me b/w Helen Reddy – Delta Dawn – 9037 (American Pie / Capitol)

Bob Welch - Sentimental Lady b/w Helen Reddy - I Am Woman – 9055 (American Pie / Capitol)

The history behind the re-recording of "I Am Woman."

Helen really never had any expectations for the song. "It clearly was not hit-single material and got no airplay at all. I used it as an opening song whenever I performed live, and it was always well received: I also noticed that the song was being singled out for mention in fan mail."

However, a little more than a year later the song was chosen to accompany the opening credits of the May 1972 Columbia films release *Stand Up and Be Counted.* A comedy film dealing with women's lib. It starred Jacqueline Bisset, Loretta Swit, Meredith Baxter and Steve Lawrence. "The decision-makers at Capitol Records thought that, in case the film was a hit, they should release 'I Am Woman' as a single." In the original version the track ran a little more than two minutes, so Helen was asked to write some additional lyrics to lengthen the song. The new verse of the song was the only mention of men ("Until I make my brother understand").

The session for the new recording took place on Sunday, April 23, 1972 and was produced by Jay Senter and engineered by Buck Herring. Jay gathered the band together at SunWest Studios located at 5533 W. Sunset Blvd Los Angeles at 7 pm. He had planned on laying down the orchestral tracks without Helen present. Helen was scheduled to arrive at 9 pm. When Helen and (then) husband-manager Jeff Wald did arrive they thought Helen would be recording with the band live as she had done with previous songs. Jeff and then Helen became angry in the control room due to the miscommunication. Jay was clearly not happy either and voices were raised by each party. Nevertheless Helen went out into the booth and overdubbed her vocals on the 16 track master tape that Jay had produced for *I am Woman* and *Don't Mess With A Woman* then she and Jeff left the studio. Immediately after that, guitarist Mike Deasy came in and played the opening riff on his 12-string electric guitar which became the signature opening sound on *I Am Woman*. Jay then asked friend, noted sax man Jim Horn, to write some string and horn charts to be recorded the following week. Afterwards Jay went into the studio with Kathy Deasy, Clydie King, Venetta Fields and Shirley Matthews and layered the background vocals.

Helen had told *Sunday Magazine* she remembered nothing about the recording session and did not know which musicians played on the song. She had in truth some of the best LA session musicians backing her, some who had worked with her earlier on recordings:

- Mike Deasy: Guitar
- Jim Horn: Woodwind / String and horns arrangement
- Jim Gordon: Drums
- Michael Melvoin: Piano
- Leland Sklar: Bass
- Dick "Slide" Hyde: Trombone
- Don Menza: Saxophone

The single was then released a month later on Monday, May 22, 1972 and triggered a five-figure payment to Helen, which at the time was sorely needed, according to Jeff. The *I Am Woman* album would follow on Monday, November 13, 1972 after some recording sessions in September and October which were held at Sound Labs.

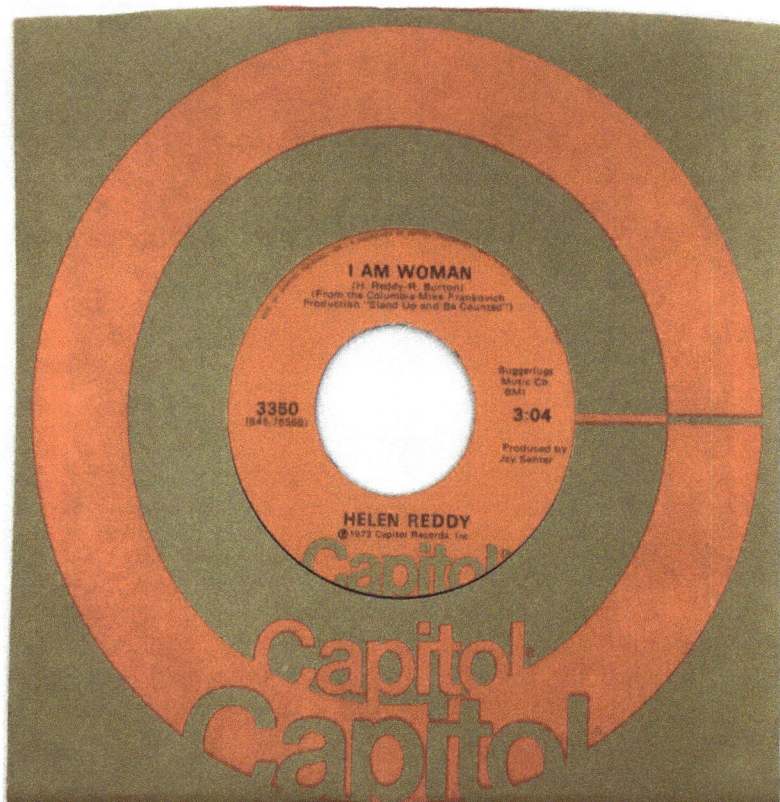

Television Appearances:

The Helen Reddy Show
(1973 NBC-TV)

This replacement series ran on NBC -TV Thursday evenings premiering on June 28, 1973 at 8 pm (7 pm Central) Some of the featured guests on the series were: Vicki Lawrence, Rod McKuen, Peter Allen, Chuck Berry, Albert Brooks, The New Seekers, Ruth Buzzi, George Carlin, Betty Wright, Cheech & Chong, Jim Croce, Mac Davis, Lee Grant, BB King, Robert Klein, Gladys Knight & The Pips,, Anne Murray, Pointer Sisters, Billy Preston, Bobby Russell, Seals and Crofts, Gloria Stein, The Temptations, Brenda Vaccaro, Paul Williams and Flip Wilson.

The Helen Reddy Special
(Air date: May 22, 1979 on ABC-TV)

This special went into rehearsals in late March and taped in early April of 1979. The guests were Jane Fonda and Elliott Gould. It was written by Bob Illes and directed by John Moffitt. Producer was Jeff Wald. Production was taped at NBC Studios, Studio 2.

An article in *Cashbox* dated April 28, 1979 read: "Reddy TV Special Now Up for Grabs in Los Angeles — Personal manager Jeff Wald is reportedly screening "The Helen Reddy Special," a television special featuring the Capitol recording artist with guest stars Jane Fonda and Elliot Gould, for both the CBS and ABC networks this week, following his purchase of the property from NBC-TV, originally slated to air the show. Wald's original deal with NBC was made prior to Fred Silverman's take over at NBC. Reddy finished taping on April 4, with expectations of a May air-date, but found the show to be scheduled to air August 21. The special, reportedly bought back from NBC for more than half a million dollars, was never seen by NBC before scheduling its network showing, claims Wald. Wald stated that Reddy was available to do interviews in the various key Nielsen markets and that she was prepared to take out ads in those same cities, but was ignored by NBC."

Note: Helen owned this special and sold copies through her official web site for several years.

TV Guide ad from the May 19th - 25th, 1979 issue

A Sampling of TV Other Appearances:

Bandstand — 1965–1966 (Australia)
The Tonight Show — 1970 – 1981 / 31 episodes
The Virginia Graham Show — July 26, 1971
Make Your Own Kind Of Music — August 31, 1971
The David Frost Show — August 25, 1971 / January 3, 1972
Love! Love! Love! TV Special — February 14, 1972
The Glen Campbell Goodtime Hour — March 14, 1972
The John Byner Comedy Hour — August 22, 1972
The Bobby Darin Show — January 26, 1973
The 15th Annual Grammy Awards — March 3, 1973
The Midnight Special (As guest / semi-regular host in 1973-1977)
1st Annual American Music Awards — February 19, 1974
The 16th Annual Grammy Awards — March 2, 1974
The Mac Davis Show — August 1, 1974 / March 27, 1975
The Glen Campbell Music Show — May 4, 1975
Some of My Best Friends Are Men — September 11, 1975
The Carol Burnett Show — September 27, 1972 / October 6, 1973 /
November 16, 1974 / November 8, 1975 / February 5, 1977 /
December 18, 1977
The Muppet Show — September 16, 1978
Sesame Street — December 1, 1978
The Love Boat — December 13, 1980
The John Davidson Show — March 19, 1981
Fantasy Island — March 6. 1982
Puttin' On The Hits — February 9, 1985
Vicki! — September 27, 1993
The Marie Show starring Marie Osmond — July 30, 2013

The Movies:

Airport 1975
(Released: October 18,1974)

Airport 1975 (also known as *Airport '75*) is a 1974 air disaster film and the first sequel to the highly successful 1970 film *Airport*. The film was directed by Jack Smight, produced by William Frye and Jennings Lang. Written by Don Ingalls. The film included stars Charlton Heston, Karen Black, George Kennedy, Linda Blair, Gloria Swanson (in her final film role) and Helen Reddy (in her first film role).

The plot revolves around two planes; a small Beechcraft with a pilot flying to Boise, Idaho on business and a Boeing 747 that was bound from East Coast to West Coast. The planes encounter a weather disturbance and are both forced to land in Salt Lake City, the Boeing ahead of the Beechcraft.

The Beechcraft pilot suffers a heart attack on approach and drops down into the Boeing's flight path striking it and tearing out most of the cockpit. The First Officer is sucked out of the gaping hole and the Flight Engineer is killed. Glass from the windows blind the pilot. No one else on-board is qualified to fly the plane. A stewardess does her best until help can be lowered from a helicopter.

Notes / Trivia:
- The film was shot on location at Salt Lake City International Airport.
- Helen was nominated for a Golden Globe for "Most Promising Newcomer – Female" for her performance.
- Helen also sang a song she wrote called "Best Friend" which appeared on her first album, but did not appear on the film's soundtrack album.
- *Airport 1975* was the seventh highest-grossing movie of 1974 in the US and Canada. With a budget of $3 million, the film grossed $47.3 million in the United States and Canada and went on to gross $55.7 million internationally for a worldwide total of $103 million.
- Available on DVD and Blu-ray.

Pete's Dragon
(Released: November 3, 1977)

Pete's Dragon is a 1977 live-action / animated musical fantasy film directed by Don Chaffey. It was produced by Jerome Courtland and Ron Miller and written by Malcolm Marmorstein. Based on an unpublished short story "Pete's Dragon and the USA (Forever After)" by Seton I. Miller and S. S. Field. The film stars Helen Reddy, Jim Dale, Mickey Rooney, Red Buttons, Jeff Conaway, Shelley Winters, Sean Marshall and the voice of Charlie Callas as Elliott.

The story, set in the early 1900s in New England, centers around a young boy named Pete (Sean Marshall) and his invisible dragon named Elliott, who run away from an abusive family, the Gogans, who purchased Pete to have him work on their farm. They arrive in Passamaquoddy Bay where the invisible Elliott creates problems and causes Pete to be labeled bad luck. Meanwhile Lampie (Mickey Rooney), the lighthouse keeper, staggers out of the local tavern and encounters Pete. Elliott then decides to make himself visible. An inebriated Lampie becomes frightened and runs into town to tell everyone what he saw ("I Saw a Dragon"). Naturally, they take this as another of his drunken illusions. His daughter, Nora (Helen Reddy), arrives. Nora leads her father back to the lighthouse and puts him to bed to sleep off his fear. Awhile later, in a seaside cave, Pete scolds Elliott for causing trouble. As they talk Nora appears. She cannot see Elliott since he turned invisible again, she warns Pete it is not safe staying in the cave because of the rising tides from the sea. She then learns he's orphaned and not from the area, so she offers him food and shelter at the lighthouse and he accepts.

Pete tells Nora of the abuse he had suffered living with the Gogans. She offers to let him spend the night at the lighthouse and they strike up a friendship ("It's Not Easy"). He learns the story of Nora's fiancé Paul, whose ship was reported lost at sea the year before. He promises to ask Elliott about Paul. Nora is of the impression that Elliott is Pete's imaginary friend.

The next morning the unqualified gypsy Dr. Terminus and his equally unqualified assistant Hoagy arrive and win over the naive townsfolk, who were initially angered by their return to the town. The local fishermen complain about the scarcity of fish and believe it's Pete's fault. Nora tells them the fishing grounds shift from time to time and Pete should be welcomed into town. She takes him to start school, where Elliott gets into all kinds of trouble and the teacher, Miss Taylor, punishes Pete unfairly for Elliott's antics. An enraged Elliott crashes through the schoolhouse, leaving his shape in the wall, as Pete runs off. Pete runs into Dr. Terminus' and refuses his offer to buy Elliott. The doctor will not be denied. Later Pete accepts Nora and Lampie's invitation to live with them permanently. When the Gogans come to town to demand him back, Nora refuses to hand him over. As the Gogans attempt to chase them in a small boat, Elliott "torpedoes" it, saving Pete ("Bill of Sale"). Dr. Terminus teams up with the Gogans to capture both Pete and Elliott and take them back to the farm. He also convinces the superstitious locals that helping him capture Elliott will solve all their problems.

That evening, a severe storm blows into the bay. From a distance a ship approaches. Dr. Terminus lures Pete to the boathouse while Hoagy does the same to Elliott. Once there, the invisible Elliott is caught in a net trap, but he frees himself, saves Pete, and confronts the Gogans. Lena yells at him, claiming Pete is their property, and waves her bill of sale at him, which Elliott torches with his fire. Now completely defenseless, they flee in fear. As he and Pete laugh, Dr. Terminus makes one more effort to harpoon Elliott, but his leg is caught in the rope and he is sent crashing through the ceiling screaming. He ends up dangling upside down near a utility pole. In a last-ditch effort, he offers to buy Elliott's "spare parts." That is denied and Elliott proceeds to destroy Dr. Terminus' traveling wagon, ending his scamming business for good.

Elliott then saves the Mayor, Miss Taylor, and the members of the Town Board from the falling utility pole, revealing himself to them. Back at the lighthouse, the lamp has been extinguished by a storm-driven wave. The ship nearing the bay is in danger of running aground and sinking. Elliott returns and lights the lamp with his own fire. As he does, Nora sees for the first time that he is indeed real. The mysterious ship is saved. The next morning, the Mayor and the townsfolk praise Elliott for his help, and Nora is reunited with Paul who had suffered amnesia the past year, and who was the sole survivor of a shipwreck at Cape Hatteras. Now that Pete has a loving family, Elliott tells him he must move on to help another child in trouble and is sad that they must part. Pete comforts Elliott by telling him if that anyone can help, he can. Elliott then happily flies away as Pete and his new family wave good-bye to him. Pete happily reminds him once again he is supposed to be invisible.

Notes / Trivia:

- Capitol Records released a single of Helen's song "Candle on the Water," with a different arrangement then that used in the film, which reached #27 on the Adult Contemporary charts.
- "Candle on the Water" was nominated for the Academy Award for Best Original Song.
- *Pete's Dragon* premiered on November 3, 1977 at Radio City Music Hall for its initial reserved seating release. The original film edit ran 134 minutes. For its general release, it was edited down to 121 minutes. When it was later re-released on March 9, 1984 it was shortened from 121 minutes to 104 minutes.
- The film's movie poster was painted by artist Paul Wenzel.
- The film was released on VHS tape in early 1980. It was re-released on VHS on October 28, 1994 as a part of the Disney Masterpiece Collection. It was scheduled to be released in the Walt Disney Gold Classic DVD Collection series on December 5, 2000, but it was pushed back to January 16, 2001.The film was re-released again in a "High-Flying Edition" DVD on August 18, 2009. That DVD includes a half-hour documentary feature, a deleted storyboard sequence, original demo recordings of the songs, and several bonus features that were included on the Gold Classic Collection release. It made its Blu-ray appearance on October 16, 2012 for the 35th-anniversary release edition.
- Production Budget in 1976 was $10 million. It grossed $18 million plus in its initial release and $4 million plus in 1984's re-release. Home video releases would bring in millions more.
- Available on DVD and Blu-ray.

Sgt. Pepper's Lonely Hearts Club Band
(Released: July 21, 1978)
Sgt. Pepper's Lonely Hearts Club Band is a 1978 musical-comedy film directed by Michael Schultz. It was written by Henry Edwards. Produced by Robert Stigwood. It starred an ensemble cast led by Peter Frampton and The Bee Gees. Helen appears in the final scene singing with a huge group of other well known celebrities. The scene was filmed on the back lot at MGM Studios on December 16, 1977.

Notes / Trivia:
- Available on DVD.

Disorderlies
(Released: August 14, 1987)
Disorderlies is a 1987 screwball comedy film starring the rap group The Fat Boys. Also stars Anthony Geary and Ralph Bellamy. The film was directed by Michael Schultz and written by Mark Feldberg and Mitchell Klebanoff. Helen plays the Happy Socialite who, while mingling at a party, smashes into a man helping another man cheating at a card game.

Notes / Trivia:
- Available on DVD.

The Perfect Host
(Sundance: January 2010 / Limited release: July 1, 2011)
The Perfect Host is a 2010 black comedy / psychological thriller film written and directed by Nick Tomnay, a remake of Tomnay's short film *The Host* (2001). The film stars David Hyde Pierce and Clayne Crawford. Helen plays Cathy Knight, Warwick's (David Hyde Pierce) curious neighbor. A small time crook who robbed a bank and is on the run talks his way into a dinner party whose host he finds out, is anything but ordinary.

Notes / Trivia:
- Filming took place in Los Angeles, California, over seventeen days.
- The film had a budget of $500,000.
- Available on DVD.

Senior Entourage (May 4, 2021)
Senior Entourage is a 2021 Mockumentary. A wickedly wild, wacky screwball-comedy featuring a cast ranging in age from 9 to 90. It's "Friends for seniors." Starring Ed Asner, Helen Reddy, Charlie Robinson, Marion Ross and Mark Rydell. Also appearing are Jamie Lee Curtis, David Lockhart and Bryant Wood.

Notes / Trivia:
- Production dates: January 20, 2017 – March 3, 2017
- Available on limited DVD.

The Woman I Am Autobiography
Penguin Books / ISBN 978-1-58542-489-4 / 2005 / 368 pages

With her 1972 song *I Am Woman,* Helen provided the ultimate feminist anthem of the 1970s. In this well written and highly anticipated memoir Helen reveals that she is so much more than the writer of one of the most widely recognized songs in history. Helen Reddy became the first Australian to win a Grammy, to have her own prime-time variety show on US television and to have three number-one hit singles in the same year.
At the height of her career, Helen's world was nearly destroyed by the death of both her parents months apart and also by the news that she had a rare, incurable disease called **Addison's disease**. In this riveting, frank and ultimately moving memoir, Helen talks about the emotional highs and lows that have shaped her as an artist and as the complex woman she was with a rich inner life sustained by a strong spiritual faith. Helen also made this book available as an audio book.

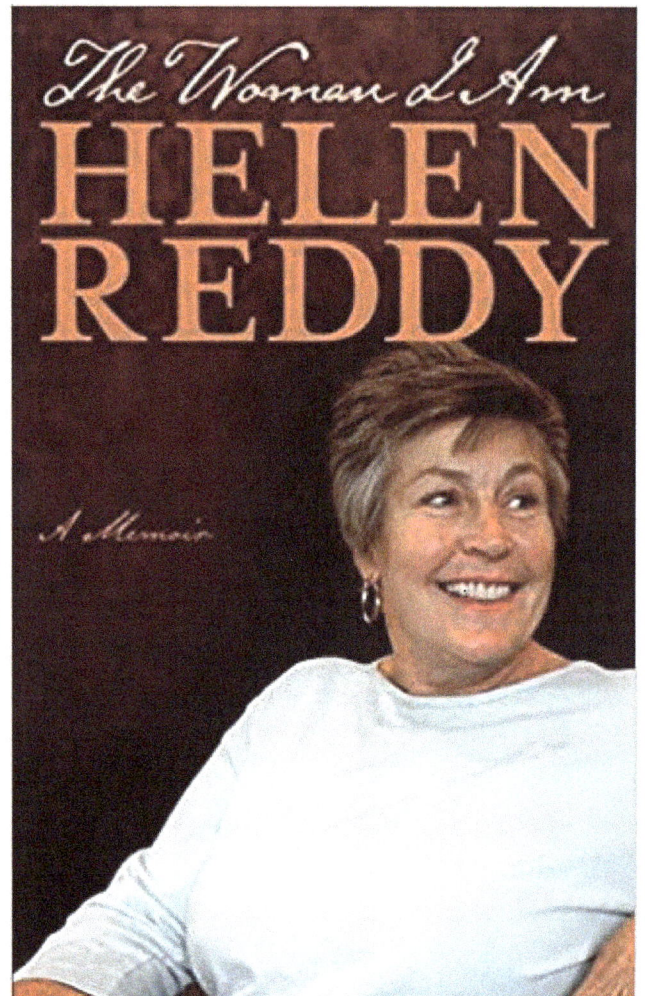

The Complete Osmond Family Illustrated Discography

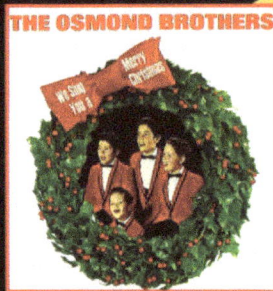

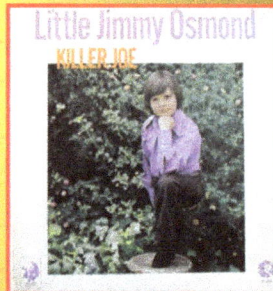

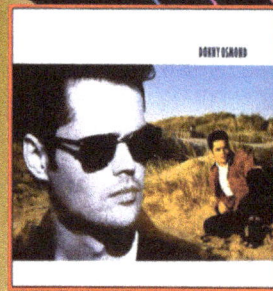

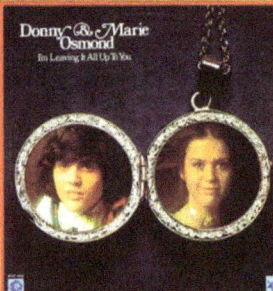

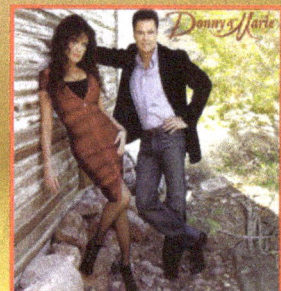

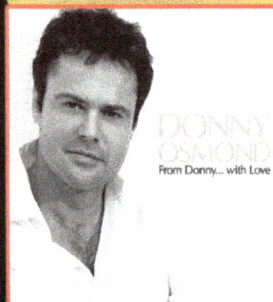

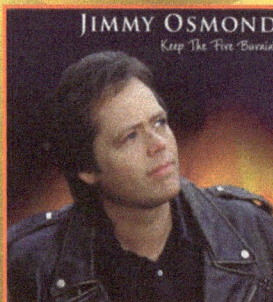

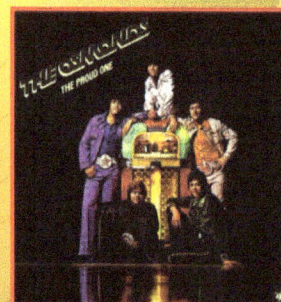

Daniel Selby

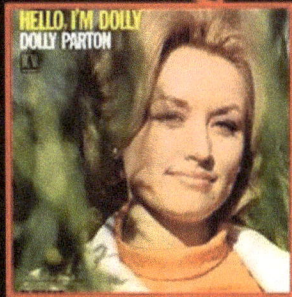

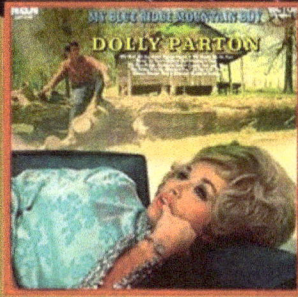

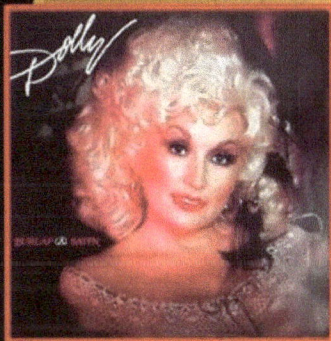

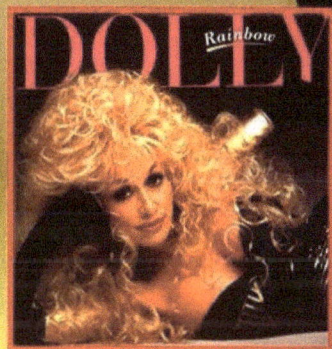

www.ingramcontent.com/pod-product-compliance
Lightning Source LLC
Chambersburg PA
CBHW061231150426
42812CB00054BA/2567